Revisiting The Challenging Counterfeit

CHRISTIANITY AND SPIRITUALISM

Steve H Hakes

Revisiting
The Challenging Counterfeit

Spiritualism and Christianity

Steve H Hakes

Paperback ISBN:	978-1-8380946-3-8
Hardback ISBN:	979-8-4384124-9-6
Kindle ISBN:	978-1-8380946-2-1
V251128125256:	mallon.detc@gmail.com

CONTENTS

Biblical Abbreviations

Ac. *Acts*
Am. *Amos*
Chr. *Chronicles*
Col. *Colossians*
Cor. *Corinthians*
Dan. *Daniel*
Dt. *Deuteronomy*
Ec. *Ecclesiastes*
Eph. *Ephesians*
Est. *Esther*
Ex. *Exodus*
Ezk. *Ezekiel*
Ezr. *Ezra*
Gal. *Galatians*
Gen. *Genesis*
Hab. *Habakkuk*
Heb. *Hebrews*
Hg. *Haggai*
Hos. *Hosea*

Is. *Isaiah*
Jas. *James*
Jg. *Judges*
Jhn. John
Jl. *Joel*
Jnh. *Jonah*
Job Job
Jos. *Joshua*
Jr. *Jeremiah*
Jude Jude
Kg. *Kings*
Lk. *Luke*
Lm. *Lamentations*
Lv. *Leviticus*
Mic. *Micah*
Mk. *Mark*
Ml. *Malachi*
Mt. *Matthew*
Nah. *Nahum*

Nb. *Numbers*
Neh. *Nehemiah*
Ob. *Obadiah*
Phm. *Philemon*
Php. *Philippians*
Pr. *Proverbs*
Ps(s). *Psalm(s)*
Pt. *Peter*
Rm. *Romans*
Ruth Ruth
Rv. *Revelation*
Sam. *Samuel*
Sg. *Song of Songs*
Ths. *Thessalonians*
Tm. *Timothy*
Tts. *Titus*
Zc. *Zechariah*
Zp. *Zephaniah*

Grades[1]

%	100-95	94-90	89-85	84-80	79-75	74-70	69-65	
Letter	A+	A	A-	B+	B	B-	C+	
Point	4.3	4	3.7	3.3	3	2.7	2.3	
%	64-60	59-55	54-50	49-45	44-40	39-27	26-14	13-00
Letter	C	C-	D+	D	D-	U+	U	U-
Point	2	1.7	1.3	1	0.7	0	0	0

---

[1]   For handier sorting in tables, I advise using A1/A2/A3 and B1/B2/B3, etc, for grade letters. I have put these here in the more familiar forms of, eg, A+/A/A- and B+/B/B-. For grade points, I round final totals to the nearest 0.5 points.

Preface

This is a book on a book. On 200906, under COVID19 lockdown I tuned in to an AoG pastor, Stephen Gaskell (Ramsbottom), preaching. He threw out an off-the-cuff warning about Spiritualism, and the thought struck me that it was high time to flag up an important yet largely forgotten book. Back in the Nineteen-seventies, I read *The Challenging Counterfeit*, by Raphael Gasson, a true Jew by ethnicity and spirituality, and a former 'Christian Spiritualist' medium.

Today the forms of Spiritualism have become more individualised, and maybe more monetised by so-called psychics. TV stations fete mediums, and hail their rescue works as helpful to the souls supposedly rescued from Earth, helpful to those rescued from them on Earth, and helpful to their own coffers. I suspect that Gasson's insights are more valuable than ever, but sadly his book is seldom available at a nice price—my 1972 Logos copy says 95¢. Should you buy a copy? Maybe my review—a stream pointing to its source—will help you decide.

For those who quite like a bit of philosophy and science, let me say that in broad terms it can help to think in three levels: the real, the counterfeit, and the counterfeit of the counterfeit. Philosophic Naturalism rules out miracles, but arguably can entertain the idea of nonmaterial spirits, both of extraterrestrial and human kinds. Nevertheless, those of an atheistic bent might wish to read the likes of Antony Flew, who, when a global teacher of atheism, considered that the scientific argument had tipped decisively in favour of affirming a transcendent deity. Flew's final book—which showed him how friendships within atheism could quickly turn sour—is, *There Is a God*. His subsequent interviews show that he had not lost his rationality—a common dismissal offered by former friends and colleagues. Conversion Therapy can cost a lot in friendships and career. Flew converted to theism (subspecies deism), but not to Christianity.

When I heard that Flew converted contrary to any wish of life beyond the grave, I thought back to an earlier convert, C S Lewis, who had reluctantly and likewise converted without any carrot of postmortal life, first to theism, and a year or so later to Christianity. C S Lewis' *Miracles*, lays out the philosophical justification of miracles, as ethically justified and rational intervention within nature, by the transcendent supernature beyond nature. It also lays out the fundamental rational objection for what Lewis called Naturalism, which to exist must both affirm and deny the absolute nature of reason, a contradiction only removed if Supernaturalism is valid, for supernature and reason are happy together. The biblical revelation proclaims this Supernature-beyond-Nature, and in which Nature has its being, to be predominantly revealed in the masculine and as personal, and, though not merely one person, for convenience the singular masculine pronoun *he* is imperfect but justified.

One might also like to read *Evolution 2.0*, by Perry Marshall, for affirmation both that life has evolved from simple to complex, and that it has evolved by built-in intelligence, given to it from the word Go: it's neither Random Evolution, nor Intelligent Design, but Intelligent Evolution. Perry's own openness to atheism's Conversion Therapy, is an interesting story in its own right.

There are many books that scratch where we itch, but let us move to *The Challenging Counterfeit*. I have never been into the occult, but over the years have read many a book on the subject.[2] I hope and pray that this book will be a useful guide to Raphael Gasson's incredible personal insights.

In comparing Bible versions, I use a simple no-fail comparative grading system, from A+ (even if they could have done better) to D- (even if they could have done worse), I have graded 10 English Bible Versions for various texts/themes: MEVV means 'My English Versions', the CEB, CEV, ERV, LEB, NABRE, NCV, NIV, NKJV, NLT, & NRSV. Some annoy me by their artificial reverential pronominal capitals (a feature going back to some C19 EVV), and by substituting God's name, Yahweh, by *the LORD*.[3] Translation is not sacrosanct, and in reading I

---

2   The related one I recommend at a semi-academic level, as distinct from Gasson's insider knowledge, is Craig S Hawkins' *Witchcraft: Exploring the World of Wicca* (2000).

3   William Tyndale pioneered ways of translating God's name, including a midway policy which most English Bible versions keep. Footnoting Ex.6:3, he said: "Iehovah is God's name...Moreover, as oft as thou seeist LORD in great letters (except there be any error in the printing) it is in Hebrew Iehovah." I prefer a consistent policy of God's name as God's name, as *Yahweh*; for some a more

often add back God's name and decapitalise. So please blame me, not the MEVV, for any inaccuracy or annoyance on these points. I've also tended to take liberties when quoting generally: for example, updating gender style, adjusting tenses, standardising abbreviations, and simplifying bibliographies intext. A man of foibles in a world of foibles.

Finally, too constant a use of "Gasson said", would weary both writer and readers. I have tried to make it clear where you're not reading his thoughts but merely mine: he was an expert; I am but a learner. And when referring to his book, for convenience I will simply use [G], followed by a page number. Chapter 14 demystifies some Christianish terms.

Steve H Hakes

---

softly softly approach works better in reinstating the idea of God's name as a name. Clearest reminders that the OT *LORD* is not the NT *lord*, offer us a doctrinal lifeline: there is more to Yahweh than Jesus, more to the uncreated society than the incarnate mode of one member.

Chapter 1

A Wandering Jew

After nine months of peaceful life, Raphael Gasson was born in London on 19200826 (ie 26th August, 1920), and died on 20150908, at Saint Mary's Hospital, Newport, on the Isle of Wight.[4] His parents were Russian Jews. His mother had had a sister named Rachel, who had died, and a near masculine equivalent name to *Rachel* was given to him, Raphael. His maternal grandparents, orthodox Judaists, had gotten into Spiritualism, hoping to regain contact with Rachel. His mother and maternal grandmother, seemingly believed that after her death Rachel had asked that her name be passed on. It probably would have been anyway in line with tradition. So, had the spirit spoken simply to stake a claim over Raphael's life?

When he was 5 y.o., a number of times his bedroom picture of her seemed to come to life. Although not as real, those who have read *The Voyage of the Dawn Treader* (C S Lewis) might imagine Reepicheep coming

---

[4]   I have integrated some details from the internet, such as http://www.christian-moral.net/pdf/raphael-gasson.pdf

from the picture into the Scrubb's home, or at least pulling faces from the frame. Raphael was terrified, the picture was hidden away, but the visitations continued. Asked about them at a séance, the spirit claimed that it had just tried to be friendly; hadn't realised that it was being fearful; and seemingly heeded the advice to back off and lie low. Why lie low? Perhaps the spirit decided that it was better to watch and wait for a better time. Or perhaps, having knocked and gained a foothold, it didn't need to keep knocking.[5] One person his parents would let knock in vain was Jesus/Yeshua,[6] and Raphael grew up with the idea that Jesus had been a false messiah, a con artist to be slagged off. However, in 1927 he saw Cecil B DeMille's film, *King of Kings*, which painted Jesus in truer light. The film challenged him to rethink, and set up some inner conflict with the separatist position in which he was brought up.

Indeed, he questioned a lot of the strictness and necessities within Judaism. Perhaps he sensed that committed to living in the past, they burdened those looking towards the future. Perhaps he picked up something of what Rich Robinson, also an ethnic Jew, would say, namely that his people's ethnolatry ("veneration by a people of themselves and their traditions"),

---

[5] G15 uses the masculine pronoun for this spirit. Whether Gasson denied that spirits could be feminine, I cannot judge.

[6] *Jesus* is the more common form of his name, but *Yeshua* is quite common within ethno-Jewish circles, and can help remind us of his ethnic, yet global, identity.

their We-Are-One slogan, had even changed Yom Kippur (Atonement Day) from God forgiving them, to them forgiving God.[7]

Raphael quested after music, and secretly practiced on a church organ within a "non-conformist" (ie free from Anglicanism) church. He would later conduct the London Philharmonic Orchestra. He admired Christianity so much that he tried to live a Christian life without becoming a Christian, believing it to be the best lifestyle to please God. He didn't see that Christians have God's direction through the messiah and his power by the Holy Spirit. Fitting into a church proved a problem, since lacking the key Jew/Judaism distinction (a useful distinction to free up ethno-Jews to upgrade from Judaism into messianism), many folk believed him to be a mismatch, perhaps a wolf in sheep's clothing—or a sheep in wolf's clothing? Sadly, he was cold-shouldered in a couple of churches, and generally faced a load of antisemitism over the years. In the early days, head down he denied being ethno-Jewish. It was a relief to discover that Spiritualism welcomed ethnic-Jews with open arms.

---

7   https://jewsforjesus.org/publications/issues/issues-vo4-no4/the-yom-kippur-dilemma. Robinson's biblical copy/paste quotes from the NIV, unsurprisingly, downgrade the scandal of God's name even from *LORD* to *Lord*, and there is polytheistic talk, yet he nicely presented a trilemma—should ethnic Jews hold to an incohesive Judaism that lacks Sinai, hold to a Western pluralism that treats religions all alike as merely subjective, or hold to Christianity as fulfilling the deific speech through messiah?

On the streets of London he saw his own 'etheric body'—as he later called it—standing in front of him as an identical twin or clone. The apparition told him to follow it, and trance-like he ended up inside what he called a Spiritualist 'church' (G19). After they sang a popular song by Clara H Scott based on Ps.119:18— "open my eyes that I may see"—the medium demonstrated her psychic powers, for starters pointing to him and telling him his name and lots more about his past experiences, his recent musical composition, and concluded by saying that he was a medium led by God into her meeting. Accepting this 'call', he sought to develop his 'psychic' abilities. Soon he was into 'deep trance' as a healing medium. That's like being figuratively dead to the world while your body is controlled by an external spirit (a 'guide').[8]

The subnatural world of visions and psychic phenomena became a normal part of his day-to-day life. It strikes me that what I call sub-nature (the diabolical), can seem more dynamic that the normal Christian life, partly perhaps because Christianity suffers from its schizophrenic divide between the ideas of cessationism and continuationism. In short, *Acts* showed apostles roaming around, with perhaps visions—certainly with spiritual experiences—being a

---

[8] In my Vampire books, I have increasingly taken to using 'divine' for something good but short of God. I now prefer talk about *deific healing* (by God/Deo), rather than *divine healing* (by a divinity). For talk of healing by fallen angels, I suggest the term diabolical/demonic healing: demons can deploy healing as fishermen can deploy bait.

---

natural every-day occurrence—naturally supernatural. Perhaps *Acts* intentionally shows us that God chooses to work in such powerful ways through those open and capable of handling it. Personally, I accept the current role of apostles/prophets within the church, and some (like pastors)[9] do see a great deal of supernatural visions and deific healing. It is likely that Raphael too reflected on the sad dearth of supernaturalism with the church, though he went on to show that it still exists.

In WW2 he worked in the Army Intelligence Corp, where he faced racial abuse, even being falsely accused of being a spy—not quite friendly fire! But within the British Army he was an effective recruitment officer for Spiritualism. The war years helped, since in the general malaise mortal life seemed cheap to many, causing many to ask questions about life beyond death. All the time, he was trying to harmonise Christianity and Spiritualism. After the war his network checked him out and gave him an official title of Spiritualist minister. Recognition can be a soul-booster.

He had a guide spirit which claimed to be from Europe. Though Raphael was a devout believer, he had hoped to verify the spirit's claim by simply having someone join a séance who would talk with it in its native language. His guide rejected that idea, as well as one to chat with a Christian minister, but allowed a

---

[9]   Coming from a rural culture, the local church leaders were often called pastors, from a Greek word that meant shepherd, looking after the 'flock' as was their duty. Biblical images for congregations vary considerably, from stones to human bodies and brides.

---

scientific test—not described—which successfully affirmed that it was an independent psyche to Raphael. He still assumed that Spiritualism was at best a Christian thing, or at least theistic, until he met up with an atheistic medium.[10]

They held a joint séance. The Rational Spiritualist didn't do God and therefore didn't do prayer or hymn singing. In fact, he claimed to practice black magic, having control spirits who were evil spirits but did good work, and thought the whole idea of being Christian a joke. Without prayers or hymns, both mediums went into the trance state, and afterwards Raphael was shocked to hear from the witnesses that his 'good' spirits had happily worked alongside the other medium's 'evil' spirits. After several more joint-séances, with similar outcomes, he wondered why on earth God was happy to work through the atheist Spiritist. But then if it wasn't God working through the black magician, who was working through he himself? Were all his trimmings of devotion, of prayer and of singing, immaterial? He had assumed that he was using the Bible biblically, but began a thorough review of it for guidance. He also tried several networks which claimed to be Christian, seeking for truth: if Spiritualism was not the whole, surely at least it was part of truth. Trying the likes of Christadelphianism, Mormonism, Roman Catholicism, and Swedenborgianism, didn't seem to help: his spirits

---

[10]   The Greek θεος/*theos* means deity/god/God: a theist believes in deity; prefixed by an α/*a*, an a-theist is someone who isn't a theist.

dismissed his search as downright silly. Then he tried a small independent Pentecostal church.

Initially, he thought that it must be a Spiritualist place, since as they prayed they spoke in foreign languages,[11] interpreted, and prophesied.[12] Alike, yet unalike, this was supernatural phenomena he hadn't met in churches. It's something that sometimes has characterised Pentecostal churches, and sometimes is seldom heard since Pentecostals have toned down in respect for visitors. While the outward phenomena seemed the same, the atmosphere seemed different.

Unaware that a Spiritualist minister was present, the exuberant pastor preached on the subject of Spiritualism, denouncing it as demonic, and obviously knew nothing about his subject other than a biblical take on it. What began as telling the pastor off, led to debate about the Bible for hours. The pastor particularly pointed out that Is.53—a chapter that

---

[11] Various translations are used for the Greek words γλωσσαις + λαλουσιν/*glōssais* + *lalousin* (1 Cor.12:30), and put simplified nowadays as a technical word as *glossolalia*. Biblically it was a fairly open wording for a phenomenon where without having learnt a language ('tongue'), Christians semi-controlled by the Holy Spirit could speak it, neither knowing what they said nor unable to control the flow. It is not by definition ecstatic, but speakers can be.

[12] While prophecy can be predictive, some argue that the general charismatic level is simply inspirational proclamation, though at times either of itself or picking up another spiritual manifestation, can reveal even the hidden hearts of the congregation.

Raphael said his race preferred to avoid—prophesied clearly about Jesus as being the messiah. In fact, Raphael didn't really believe that Scripture was directly inspired and formed by God, so predictive prophecy had seemed to him to be no more than educated guesses—in the order of Jules Verne. Nevertheless, the pastor lined up many scriptures from the Bible, that all dovetailed into the birth, life, and death, of Jesus. There seemed to be simply too much coincidence and detail to avoid the implication that predictive prophecy was valid, and that Jesus had been the prophesied messiah. If there is specific reliability, perhaps there is general reliability? If the Bible's predictive prophecy was valid, what about the rest of it, such as its apparent condemnation of Spiritualism?

At his next and last séance, his guide spirits turned murderous, and he couldn't understand why. A few days later, on 470607, he attended an Elim[13] church, and he was thrilled with the idea carried in a song: that he could have a blessed assurance that Jesus was personally his. During the singing of that song, he invited Jesus to make it so. He felt a new type of spirituality, and hoped it would make him a better medium. His spirits weren't so chuffed, and feeling that perhaps they were right he decided to chuck them and rethink Spiritualism.

---

[13]   Church:Elim is part of the Pentecostal section of Christianity.

He was water-baptised on 470903 (ie 3rd. Sep. 1947) in Clapham, and on 470930 was spirit-baptised.[14] Finally convinced that Spiritualism was evil under the hood, and beginning to denounce it, he found himself under spiritual attack. In public, extreme dizzy spells attacked whenever he tried to denounce Spiritualism. In private, sleepy spells attacked, seemingly to force him into deep trance and into suicide. Through prayer and biblical education, he formed a defence against those attacks, and learnt how to move from defensive to offensive.

His family had intended him to become a rabbi—an ethno-Jewish term for *teacher*. Rabbi Yeshua warned not against the term—his disciples used it of him (Mk.9:5)—but against abusing it as a badge of pride: all were learners before the ultimately teacher (Mt.23:7-8). Gasson did in fact become a Christian/Messianic rabbi. He also worked as a secular teacher/rabbi in various

---

14   Baptism is basically an immersion, although some argue that even if immersion is ideal for water, sprinkling can be as valid and might be more practicable. In biblical circles, water is used to dramatise the inner reality of conversion, and has lots of associated ideas, such as a public career-jeopardising commitment of loyalty to Christ. Spirit-baptism is when the Holy Spirit unlocks an added dimension to Christian life. Some deny that it ever applied as such. Some simply deny that it now applies. Some who affirm it as current add that it opens the door to many spiritual manifestations. I agree that it can encourage folk to access such manifestations, but disagree with the 'gateway to power' idea, for most of the spiritual manifestations were active before spirit-baptism (eg the prophets under Sinai).

UK and CI schools, and achieved multiple doctorates. He married twice: Eva Patricia in 1949–2011 (died); Iris 2012. He received an MBE in 2002. Perhaps because having been ethnically Jewish—which carried its own problems throughout his mortal years—against his express wishes his body was cremated in a non-Christian setting.

∞

Interesting though his book undoubtedly is, his aim was not to interest but to direct away from the froth and bubble of the psychic, and towards the rock of true spirituality. He began with Is.53:6: "All of us, like sheep, have strayed away. We have left God's paths to follow our own. Yet Yahweh laid on him the sins of us all" (NLT).[15] Isaiah's 'us' referred to the disloyal straying—like sheep from their shepherd—from the covenant of Sinai that still applied to Isaiah's fellow Jews. Today the term *Jew* is generally taken—as it was by Raphael—as both an ethnicity (which it is) and a religion (which it is not), and the term *Israelite* assumed to be identical (it is not).

Biblically, all Jews were Israelites, but not all Israelites were Jews: Moses was not a Jew; Abraham was not an Israelite. Similarly, all folk born in Yorkshire are English, but not all born in England are Yorkshire folk. He wished to say from the start, both that he, as an

---

[15]   The KJV was used throughout. The RSV would have improved, but in those days it generated some Bible rage, making some hesitant to use it. Nowadays biblical quotes should at least be taken from the usually good NKJV, to which many happily moved from the KJV.

ethnic Jew, had wandered, [16] and that Yahweh had provided at-one-ment (Yom Kippur) through Yeshua the messiah. He learned the last lesson the hard way. Indeed, he had struggled between facts and theories, and knew how we can prefer to keep pet theories over cold facts. Is this through a sense of ownership, the feeling that facts should keep their grubby hands off my theories? We can feel that someone else's theory/idea is threatening ours, violating our space.

He spoke to the 'Church of Christ' (G12), meaning the whole global church, not simply to some denomination within the world-wide church, and he included the caution that even true Christians were not immune to the seduction of Spiritualism. Indeed, Gasson's second chapter underlines that the term Spiritualism is not strictly true, since that Movement has to do with spirits, rather than with the spiritual.

I think he sometimes underplayed the trinity. For instance, he referred to Christ not simply as saviour

---

[16]   Whether Gasson had wandered from the covenant of Sinai depends of course on whether that covenant still existed. Disagreeing that it did, I agree that he had wandered from the remnants of Sinai as *per* Judaism. In another sense, some say that all non-Christians are prodigals (Lk.15) who may return home, strayed sheep returned back into the fold. Before living memory humanity (not us) strayed—perhaps like the prodigal. Say rather that when pre-Christians we had never *left* God's home since it has never *been* our home—we were never *in* his flock so never strayed *from* it. Under Moses the children of Israel did not *return* home, but Canaan *became* their home.

but as the lord who should run our lives. Sure, the NT's (New Testament's) emphasis of lord is on Jesus, but in some contexts we might prefer to factor in the trinity, since our father is ultimate lord, our brother is strategic lord, and our helper is tactical lord, though in unity there is one lordship.[17] There is a lordship in industry over useful tools, but God's lordship, besides being rightful, is purely for our benefit, so his lordship over us is a thing for thanks, not for regret. Gasson was a trinitarian, and spoke of depending on God, surrendering to Christ, and being enabled by the spirit. Overall, he called God "my god", to indicate a personal relationship between himself and God (G13): here I commend what he said not how he said it.

---

[17]   The Athanasian Creed says that "the Father is lord, the Son is lord, and the Holy Spirit is lord....yet not three lords, but one lord."

Chapter 2

D is For...

What is Spiritism, which Christianity and Spiritualism condemns, and why can Spiritualists believe that they are on the side of the angels? The short answer is that Spiritism simply runs on spirits that are neither of God nor good. Gasson tended to deem Spiritualism—he used that term simply for convenience—to be a long prophesied interaction with evil spirits, set up by evil spirits. He cited 1 Tm.4:1: "The spirit clearly says that in later times some will turn away from what we believe, by paying attention to spirits that deceive and to what demons teach." I suspect that Gasson held 'later times' to mean a later part of the church age, our 'Psychic Age', so to speak, rather than the season following Sinai, the church age. Throughout the church age some have departed from truth, and I think Paul's immediate concern was to advise Timothy to shoot down such nonsense in Ephesus (1 Tm.1:3-5).

The human desire to reconnect with those we have loved and lost, indeed to believe that they are not lost, can be very strong. Spiritualism's claims to look beyond death can seduce our curiosity. Some sincerely seek a closer walk with God, misunderstanding that

Spiritualism takes away from, not towards, him. Texts such as Lv.20:27 can indicate what was wrong then, and is wrong now. Bear in mind, however, that such penalties under the Covenant of Sinai were political in nature, aimed at preserving covenant loyalty against treason within the nation that had yet to fulfil its mission: the unhatched egg required special handling. Now hatched, such penalties have ended with Sinai. It was once perfectly justified to terminate as traitors those who wilfully violated certain important rules and thereby violated their community and their mission. Termination—expressed as cutting off, as death— could rightfully pan out as social, rather than as physical, death. For instance, Joseph considered divorcing, not executing, his wife for adultery, and was called righteous (Mt.1:19). Exile was a form of death. Some slander God by taking what was an important interim stage for the global egg, and universalising it as if a bloodbath by a batty and berserk deity—the covenant context is key. To jump from 'it mattered then', to 'it doesn't matter now', is likewise a jump where one should look before they leap. Some principles still matter (murder remains wrong); some customs do not (physical circumcision is superseded by spiritual circumcision): biblical judgement is required.

The spirits speak both nicely and misleadingly about God, and their 'god' is one who blinds against messianic light (2 Cor.4:4; Eph.2:2), not God. Some branches of Spiritualism deny theism. If Spiritualism was godly, would the spirits not teach all branches the fundament stem of belief, since the spirit world surely knows that God is and deserves honour? Likewise, if the spirit world knows that the concept, God, is invalid, would it not teach atheism throughout the Movement? Why should the same spirits accommodate both theism and atheism, as if neither position, nor truth, really mattered? *The Banner of Light* (1865₁₁04) claimed the devil as the spirits' father.

Spiritualism claims that it has proof of survival after death, and that the church only has faith/hope of such. However, all it proves is that spirits exist which claim to be the deceased. Christian faith is in he who proved life beyond death by his resurrection. We might add that Christianity talks not of survival beyond death, but of resurrection to a glorified life very different from the continuation of the mortal pursuits, friendships, and family trees, so useful in mortal life, even as birth life is very different to embryonic life. Gasson correctly noted that *per* the Bible, contact with the deceased isn't normal. He also threw in a bit of Ec.9:5. Was he saying that those who have died don't exist? No.

It was exhortation. To the Preacher's mind, "the living know that they will die" (Ec.9:5), so unlike the dead have opportunity on earth to shape their lives in the light of eternity, whereas when it comes to facing the loves and hates and envies of earthly life, the dead, having moved beyond the picture they were once within, no longer know it. And while worldly feasting and fun are recommended in measure, for spiritual development the house of mourning can teach us better than the house of feasting (7:2). This sense of *shaping*—if not of *choosing* destination—carries into the NT.

But might Spiritualism's 'proof' be phoney, if mediums play to the incredulity of their clients? Well yes, but overall Gasson spoke of three levels of phenomena: the genuine, the counterfeit, and the counterfeit of the counterfeit. The latter is a fake of Spiritualism; Spiritualism is a fake of God's interactions, True Spirituality. Somewhat similarly, the NT speaks of the pneumatic (the spiritual level), the psychic (the soulish level), and the physic (the physical level).[18] Christianity, operating at the highest level, incorporates all the levels of human life. Gasson underlined that Spiritualism has resulted in severe tragedy for many, and that his release from it came through God. He did argue that Spiritualism's 'proof' was phoney, but in the sense that demons merely played to the incredulity of their honest mediums.

From the (wrong) perspective of Spiritualism, on the one hand Spiritism is evil, but Spiritualism is a good which obligates all Spiritualists to promote it as an ethical duty, a glorious truth. Spiritualism holds that spirits use physical bodies on Earth, and like a snake shedding a skin, discard the physical skin at death for a psychical body, but, at least for a while, can remain interactive with Earth. Where the spirits came from in the first place is probably a question that different Spiritualists speculate about: Christians likewise have differing ideas. I suspect that though they minimalise death, a flat denial of death overstates their case. Perhaps Gasson too quickly tucked Spiritualism into the procrustean bed of Gen.3:4, and limited that biblical text to physical death.

---

[18]   This is rough picture language, used widely by Christian advocates of Trichotomy.

Innumerable times he praised Spiritualists at large, as loudly as he condemned Spiritualism *in toto*. He described them as usually decent, honest (in intention), in some limited sense 'spiritual', joyful, and sincere. But though they believe that they need not fear death, they lack God's life and remain in the dark. His warnings to Christians can, in this light, pan out as urging Christians to know Jesus dynamically, not statically, daily as the road, not merely the once upon a time entrance to the road.[19]

The lack of spiritual discernment he found disturbing, and he lamented that a Christian rally had happily invited Spiritualists into their ranks. Even Spiritualists seek to be more discerning. To them, Spiritists include those who merely dabble in Spiritualism for kicks and for selfish ends, 'believers' when it suits them. In short, Spiritualists who take the spiritual out of Spiritualism are likened to weed among the wheat, weed perhaps demon-controlled. I think this last idea is of people who, as spirits in physical bodies, are considered to be more at home with those departed spirits who remained in the evils of selfishness.

---

[19]   It seems to me that he used the term 'lord' of God, then of Jesus, then called Jesus 'lord of all' (G38). I deem it wiser to follow Paul's general method in not calling God 'lord', so as to keep the distinction of two separate persons: the father is not the son; the son is not the father. 'Lord of all', used of Jesus, biblically means that the pan-ethnic lord redemptively and instantly unites all those who, whether ethnically Jews or not, turn to him. Its meaning is different in the OT, where Yahweh is lord of all the Earth in sovereignty (Ps.97:5).

From background ideas—such as spirits seeking worship through idols (2 Kg.17:12), and Satan bargaining with Yeshua for his worship (Mt.4:9)—Gasson suggested that in order to gain worship from selfish humanity, Satan has created Spiritualism to pander to human selfishness, so as to gain indirect worship. Perhaps. Or Satan might simply seek to redirect worship from God so that we lose out, not that he gains. God only seeks worship for our sakes, not his— he is neither a needy 'god' nor any type of 'god'.

Gasson described Spiritualism as seeming good, its phenomena and ideas as fascinating, as real as heaven and hell, and yet demonic.[20] He warned that even spying on the fascinating can capture us.[21] It's wiser to see it from the biblical portal, than within its own. And it is wiser all round for the church to deliver the biblical goods, rather than leave it to the Spiritualists to offer counterfeit goods on the black market.

Having contrasted between how Spiritualists deem Spiritists, Gasson contrasted how active Pentecostal Christians can deem inactive Christians.[22] It seems like

---

[20] Some might ridicule the idea of hell (and perhaps even heaven) being real. If they mean real *places*, I tend to agree; if they mean real *dimensions*, I disagree.

[21] I think of Sallowpad the Raven's "easily in but not easily out, as the lobster said in the lobster pot!" (C S Lewis). In *The Lord of the Rings* (J R R Tolkien), when Frodo saw the evil glowing tower of Minas Mogul, he was overcome by allure and ran towards it.

[22] Gasson spoke here of "the Great Jehovah", a phrase sometimes sung. The name 'Jehovah' was in fact a medieval mishmash of God's name. Most agree that the

enough that the primitive church was much more on fire than the sophisticated and cerebral church in the west. Once, occult books were ousted by Bibles (Ac.19:19). Today, we might more readily read of Bibles being ousted by occult books—certainly on public bookshelves. Gasson concluded this chapter by reference to what many call spiritual warfare, referring to Eph.6:10-8.[23] But before turning to the weapons Spiritualism uses, he turned to how it began its army.

biblical name is *Yahweh*, and that it was used almost 7,000 times in the Old Testament as we have it. Comparative grades: LEB (A+); ERV (D+); NABRE/NLT (D); CEB/CEV/NCV/NIV/NKJV/NRSV (D-).

[23] Don't be too pedantic. Roman had military knowhow to take and to keep turf. In 1 Ths.5:8 Paul referred to "faith and love"—not "righteousness"—"as a breastplate", and to put on "the hope of salvation"—not "salvation"—"as a helmet".

Chapter 3

The Tale of Two Foxes

Gasson said that spirits had waited long for a couple of simple teenage girls—the Fox sisters—to begin in 1848. That is, in Western culture the modern movement with certain exclusive features, called Spiritualism, began with them. But it was not without antecedent, and he also called it a revival, a form of witchcraft. This chapter shocked me a little, for I was (and remain) a fan of Sir Arthur Conan Doyle's *Sherlock Holmes* stories. Commendably in *The Adventure of the Sussex Vampire* (1924), Holmes says to Dr Watson that their "agency stands flat-footed upon the ground, and there it must remain. The world is big enough for us. No ghosts need apply." Our floors should resist hell, but our roofs should be open to God. But wherever he lived, Sir Arthur, howbeit deceived in his own homes,[24] happily kept his Spiritualism out of his Holmes.

---

[24] It seems that he gullibly defended some fakes as being genuine. Perhaps his gullibility here was because he had met genuine Spiritualism, preferred to err on the side of caution before dismissing claims to genuineness, and was reluctant to admit to misjudgements. In *The Devil's Foot*, Holmes assumed that like himself, Dr Watson was

---

In the history of demons, I do not think that we need to take the word of 'guide spirits' that claim human etiology. I suspect that whenever the universe began, they were either created outside space-time, or within it from the start. As to the 'problem' of Spiritualism waiting so long to emerge, I have no more a problem with thinking in terms of seasons, than I have with C20 Pentecostalism beginning in its own season. Both show antecedent forms throughout the millennia.

As to Margaret and Kate Fox, they were born to Methodist parents in New York State. Recently moved to a new tenancy, they soon heard strange knockings and furniture being moved around, and felt vibrations that shook them in their beds. Before long Kate could snap her fingers and be answered by a knock of unseen knuckles. Some church leaders bought into the idea of spirits of deceased humans trying to make contact. The girls became longterm mediums, but came to unhappy ends. Gasson said that they had become drunks with low morals. Finding Spiritualism to be a lie, they cursed God as they died. This is suggestive but not conclusive. After all, good folk have for bad reasons, become disillusioned about good causes (2 Tm.4:10). But I would have liked to have read a happy ending, that having lived unhappily they had died well.

In 1852, a Mrs Hayden introduced Spiritualism to England. Soon it had its own newspaper, *The Yorkshire Spiritual Telegraph*. The buzz increased. Some mediums proved better than others at achieving

---

not "prepared to admit diabolical intrusions into the affairs of men". But we must see that the demonic exists.

---

physical healing, sometimes offered 'freely': healings included such as physical healing from blindness. But Gasson underlined that what is cashless to the pocket, can be costly to the soul: "pseudo-christs and pseudo-prophets will come and perform great signs and wonders to lead astray, if possible, even God's chosen ones" (Mt.24:24). Paying for the deception includes losing, or never gaining, spiritual insights, such as the deificity[25] of messiah;[26] the atonement (at-one-ment) for us that Jesus accomplished by being killed for us; the existence of hell;[27] the existence of nonhuman spirits hostile to humanity (demons); the reliability of the Bible; and humanity's deep-seated hostility towards submission to God.

I agree that such losses are true losses, but I think that Gasson overrated Spiritualism as being that which ancient scriptures warned against. For instance, I think

[25] G51 used 'divinity', but meant more than that word sometimes means.

[26] Systematic formulation of this idea from unsystematic biblical data, is difficult, for several truths are in tension. In ascribing deity to God's eternal son, we must neither deny deity to the father nor to the spirit. In ascribing deificity to God's son *as incarnate*, we must neither deny humanity nor limitation to him: Jesus is the permanent temporal mode of the uncreated second person of deity.

[27] Some prefer the term *hades*. I suggest that in some sense hell begins on Earth, in its sense of being cut off from God, even from Christianity, and will become permanent after death for those who basically want nothing to do with God. The bearability of hell is another study area.

he was wrong to take 1 Tm.4:3's "forbidding marriage", to mean Spiritualism's 'twin-soul/flame' disloyalty/ divorce idea.[28] 'Twin-souling'—the idea of a destined 'soulmate'—basically teaches that each person has their perfect twin whom they should/ought marry (OK, less emphasis on marriage nowadays), and that if they marry before discovering—by a guide spirit—their *soulmate*, then they are fully justified—perhaps even obliged—to replace their spouse (and any family) with their *soulmate*, thereby debasing marriage. It is dead wrong. It is diabolically wrong. It is immoral.[29] But it prescribed marriage—to ones' *soulmate*—rather than proscribed marriage: hardly Paul's target.

In speaking of medieval witchcraft, Gasson gave a figure of 30,000. It seems that sentenced as witches (about 1/5 were men)—between "30,000 to 50,000...during the 400 years from 1400 to 1800"—were executed, sometimes falsely (Irvin & Sunquist's *History of the World Christian Movement* vi (2001:343)).[30] His point was that

---

28   Paul's line applied initially to C1 Ephesus. Even today, pseudo-Christian influencers can try to remove the moral norm of marriage, wishing their sin to seem sinless as they 'live with' 'partners' while it suits them. The latter seasons (1 Tm.4:1) had begun; Timothy wasn't to be surprised; nor should we be.

29   Perhaps the nearest Christian equivalent is 1 Cor.7:15, but that encouraged Christians to expedite, but never to initiate, a divorce where their spouse had resolutely rejected them and Christ.

30   Some politically inflate the figure to as many as 9 million (see Sandra Miesel:

---

nonhuman phenomena, some spirit-virus type plague, must have been disturbing the natural world to have created such a backlash. Even England's King James wrote about demonism. Whether or not medieval herbalism and witchcraft stood shoulder to shoulder with today's Spiritualism, contact with demonic spirits has doubtless always been going on.

In contrasting Spiritualism's downrating of Jesus' death, Gasson quoted Rm.8:1—from the KJV. Let's note that this is one of those texts where the KJV should be decluttered of centuries of lite scribal comments embedded within its underlying text. Paul spoke here of κατακριμα/*katakrima*, as freedom from ultimate condemnation, independent of our level of holiness. Gasson's basic point stands: that a level of forgiveness beyond human comprehension comes from the father only through Jesus, by the spirit. It's not flippant—as if we should sin more and merrily as if God benignly forgives all. It's not self-delusional. It's a package reality of God's verdict of *forgiven*, which includes God's intervention in change, so that even the adulterous are transformed out of that reality into the new creation reality, even though they can slide back into—and so be rightly condemned *in this life*—the ways of their former nature.[31] Spiritualism underplays spiritual intervention from above.

He covered a few Spiritualist networks in this chapter, looking at some of their main beliefs and outlooks.

---

www.crisismagazine.com/october2001/feature1.htm (2006)).

[31]   See Jean Darnall's *Life in the Overlap*.

Although they might claim not to be antagonistic to any religious beliefs, he vigorously disputed that claim, besides arguing that Christianity should be antagonistic towards Spiritualism! [32] In 1937 Anglicanism, under Dr. W C G Lang (Archbishop of Canterbury), investigated Spiritualism, seeking different viewpoints, and even questioning the spirits. I have read what on the internet claims to be that report. My take was that it basically allowed that although Spiritualism at best helped fill in a belief-hole within Christianity, namely the 'communion of the saints', it was otherwise imperfect and flawed, a wandering sheep needing an Anglican shepherd. Only one passing mention was made of the idea of demonic spirits, quickly drowned out by the idea that maybe it had more divine than demonic spirits. A sort of 'don't deny the bad stuff; won't deny the good stuff; good stuff can't come from bad stuff.'

The *Psychic Press* had a field day in badmouthing stuffy Anglicanism for not making the Report public. Gasson presumed that the Report would never be officially lodged, for better or worse, in the public domain. He suspected that the Report was favourable to Spiritualism's central position, since several members of the investigating Committee were already in Spiritualism's camp.

---

[32]   1 Cor.10:21: "you cannot drink from the cup of the lord and from the cup of demons, too. You cannot eat at the lord's table and at the table of demons, too" (NLT—modified).

Before gaining recognition as a religion, mediums could be prosecuted either as true (under a Witchcraft Act), or as false (under a Vagrancy Act); for either truly conjuring up spirits which falsely claimed to be deceased, or for falsely claiming to have conjured up spirits; for breathing, or for not breathing—Catch 22. The judicial rule of thumb was perhaps to ignore them if they kept a low profile, so suppressing the Movement by self-censorship. With more freedom from prosecution has come more public access, and perhaps bolder visions. Gasson reported a strong urge within Spiritualism for globalisation of politics and a global Police Force, and again lamented how lukewarm so many Christians were in comparison, failing to please the father of lights—a reference to God having created the starry lights (KJV: Jas.1:17).

Chapter 4

Spiritualism and Christians

His next chapter begins with a quotation from Mt.7:21: "Not everyone who calls me their lord will get into the kingdom of heaven. Only the ones who obey my father in heaven will get in."[33] Followers of false christs can genuinely believe that they are following the true christ (Gasson was once a pseudo-Christian: G17). But was Jesus' context about the eternal kingdom still to come, or about the interim messianic kingdom that was then soon to come, which is his church? I ask this in disagreement to Gasson's stated belief that everyone into Christian Spiritualism is under sentence of eternal damnation unless they repent.

I believe that Spiritualism can damn folk *within*, but not *beyond*, mortal life. Christian Spiritualism is the branch that makes most of the idea that what Jesus did, it does, so believing that it follows him as lord, lord. It does not affirm him as God's one-of-a-kind,

---

[33] CEV—modified. I suggest that here Jesus spoke about the messianic kingdom began by his resurrection, and that the father's will was the entrance ticket of welcoming his son (Jhn.6:29).

son, insisting merely that he was an outstanding medium and teacher in ethics, at least given his cultural norms and limitations. It's easy enough to see that Christian Spiritualists can twist many biblical ideas, but defending Christ's virgin conception raises all sorts of questions.

On one Spiritualist forum I looked at while writing this book, one Christian Spiritualist was basically warned by Admin to cool it, and definitely not to preach it! His point was that God is able to work miracles, so why not virgin birth as he believed, although he added the idea that maybe (because of Isaiah's Hebrew, not Matthew's Greek)[34] it was simply birth by a young woman. I was tempted to ask him that if indeed Jesus was born of a virgin (which I believe), then why had God supernaturally intervened in nature to produce yet one more medium? It is a dangerous question within

---

[34]   All the MEVV agree that Matthew's use of the Greek meant 'virgin'. I've graded the Incarnation texts, Is.7:14; Mt.1:25; & Lk.2:33.

Since Isaiah spoke centuries before Christ's birth of a sign that his king would see, unless Isaiah meant a previous virgin birth to Christ's, then he meant something along the lines of a then unwed woman who would soon conceive a honeymoon son whose birth would start a prophetic clock ticking. The Hebrew could mean 'virgin' but is better as 'young/unwed' woman.

In the nature of prophecy a deeper meaning of a deeper birth (*viz* virgin birth) lay hidden, and Matthew brought this out about he who was "God with us" in a deeper way than the child in King Ahaz' time. Comparative grades: NRSV (A+); ERV (A); CEB/NABRE (B+); CEV/LEB/NCV/NIV/NLT (B-); NKJV (D-).

Spiritualism because it raises the dangerous answer that Jesus was/is more than, perhaps other than, a mere medium, perhaps even deity himself. I can see why Admin sounded alarm bells.

'Born again' (G62)—technically implying reincarnation—has become a holy cow within Evangelicalism. Translation aside, Jesus' 'born anew' (γεννηθη ανωθεν/gennēthē anōthen) gets twisted in Spiritualist circles into being about turning over a new leaf, about making good for past wrongs, and about doing better in the future. Gasson finally saw that it meant much much more.

The eucharist for Spiritualists means a thankfulness for Jesus' life and example—one might ask why his disciples never wrote a manual for mediums. That his blood was shed and his body given over to execution, is simply sad, they say. Some incorporate a eucharistic service on Sundays, dwelling on Christ's love—a great theme. Their services by and large are warm and friendly, prayful and reverent. Gasson lamented that besides Christian Spiritualism not preaching Christ's atonement for us, neither did he hear of it in the various Christian-identity denominations he visited, until Elim. He begged the church to put its house in order on this issue. Yes, but I question whether one or two he visited, were part of Christ's church.

Some blind Christian guides even flew the Spiritualist flag with pride, and he named and shamed various Anglicans, warning that even true sheep can become wolves. True, and let it be added that wolves can be paid to watch over the flock and to wear dog collars: Anglicanism is neither a safe house nor guarantees

Christianity. Not even the good works of the *Greater World Christian Spiritualist League* and similar, should gain them the Christian vote. From their creedal statements we can see that the devil is not in the details but is totally hidden.

Gasson mentioned a belief that animals have the same kind of soul as humans. [35] That belief can lead to ethically putting the life of an aunt on par with the life of an ant. That could either mean that the ant's life is deemed to be as equally meaningful as the aunt's, or that the aunt's life is deemed to be as equally meaningless as the ant's. And so, other things being equal, saving two ants might be deemed morally better than saving one aunt—which could be difficult to explain to the uncle.

Naturally we should not decide beliefs on how easy or how hard they can be to fit in with ethics, but it is worth bearing in mind that wrong ethical decisions can stem from misinformation: right facts matter. Some teach—officially or otherwise—reincarnation, though strictly speaking the belief in every animal being an embodied soul, does not require the idea, transmigration. Gasson often urged his readers to act aright, but to pray aright I would caution against his exhortations to ask the lord (G67)—that road leads to Sabellius. Ask God the father through the lord.

---

[35]   The primary biblical differentiation is the expression, *God's image*, being exclusively for mankind. Soul, in its sense of personality, is a biblical given, as is a general care of animals, but personality can exist below the level of personhood.

Chapter 5

Sunday School Spiritualists

Their schools for youngsters are named Lyceums, after the temple dedicated to the Greek divinity, Apollo Lykaios (Apollo, master over wolves). That temple, in Athens, soon became enlarged to be a place of philosophy, hosting names such as Socrates, Plato, and Aristotle. The teaching system was introduced by A J Davis (b.1826), a bright lad from less than bright parents. Somewhat out of the blue he wrote a book on philosophy, perhaps guided by demonic spirits which he called angels. He soon became a strong psychic, having X-ray vision through which he could see infected human organs as dim compared to healthy surrounding organs. (When a medium, Gasson likewise had this ability and could diagnose types of bone problems.)

In 1884 Davis seemingly had an out of body experience (OOBE), seemingly speaking with Emanuel Swedenborg (dec'd). Gasson mentioned both as facts. I can accept that OOBE might be factual,[36] but I very

---

[36]   Either part of the mind actually leaves the physical brain (sometimes said to occur with near-death experiences: NDE), or a third party inputs directly into

much doubt whether Davis spoke to the real Swedenborg—Gasson was generally at pains to explain that at séances people met demons impersonating the deceased, not the deceased themselves.

Davis seemingly, through predictive prophecy, saw typewriters and petrol cars. As to whether demons can thus foresee the future, I am in doubt. Gasson himself mentioned secular predictors such as Jules Verne, who could extrapolate from what was to what could later be. Some say that the mobile/cellphone was foreseen by Star Trek *communicators*.

Gasson spoke of God vainly giving Davis time beyond his 'allotted time' to repent, though Davis died without salvation. The idea of allotted time was a traditional idea that 70 years was man's standard allotment. But if we say that to live longer shows God's grace, do we not *ipso facto* say that to live less shows God's curse? Ps.90:10 reflected the situation of the exodus, in which most adults who had left Egypt, were condemned to die before Canaan: 70-80 years was a figure of speech for the condemnation of them to an early grave. Adding to symbolism (where a complete life was symbolized by the number of fullness, 7—multiplied by 10 for realism) an extra year—again multiplied by 10— underlined the frailty of mortal life compared to Yahweh, to whom a millennium was like a day (v4). I doubt that God has set either general or specific times for folk to die, let alone decreasing or increasing such times. If we are careful in life and generally live in a

---

the imagination along the lines of virtual reality—X-ray vision could also be direct brain input.

---

careful society, then other things being equal, we will meet death later than if we are careless and live in a careless society. I'm unconvinced that Davis died without a saviour. Demons can keep people in the dark in mortal years, but demons can't, I believe, keep people from the light in immortal time—they simply enjoy leading the blind.[37]

Davis' name is honoured by the Lyceum Movement. He claimed to have been to 'Summerland', where spirit children attend the spirit-world school. He explained in 1863 how he would set this up for mortal children, and was quickly given the job as conductor/leader. A Mr J Burns introduced this system to the UK. Quite a lot of historical facts and figures are given.[38] Of more interest perhaps, is the fact that Lyceums were popular with kids. I wonder how church Sunday Schools compare. What were the Summerland factors?

The names were kiddie friendly: in Summerland there were districts called Crystal Lake, Rock Nook, Happy Valley, etc, with ideas such as people who died in infancy after illnesses, going to the Crystal Lake to recuperate, and apparently growing up under spirit guides much the same way that they would have grown up had they not died, a parallel reality, so to speak. The Lyceums are not for Bible study, but for

---

[37] For my position on inexclusivism, see my *Salvation Now and Life Beyond*.

[38] One mistake on G75 is purely grammatical: [it's manager] means [it is manager]—the possessive case lacks the apostrophe, so it should have been read [its manager]. A simple typo.

Summerland study, the vision of Davis. An emphasis is put on discussion, not mere teaching from the front. Learning stages—or growth stages—are twelve in number, a mix of age and progress. First, Fountain Group (level 1: beginners), then Stream, River, Lake, Sea, and Ocean, after which one can attain to seeing the Beacon, Shore, Banner of Progress, and New Star, after which an Aspiring Excelsior enters the heart, leading finally to Group 12, Liberty.

Liberty? Lyceums don't teach Jesus as the one-of-a-kind messiah. Now "what the messiah has freed us for is freedom!" (Gal.5:1), meaning entry into the messianic age of messiah's kingdom, begun by messiah's death and granted by God's free favour—irrespective of good works and the covenant of Sinai. This is the truth which by his spirit sets people free (Jhn.8:32).

Religious and philosophical excerpts from a broad range of mankind are used, then a Silver Chain (a poem on ethics), a bit of song reflection, then a Golden Chain (a discussion on spirit manifestations, common humanity, insights into Spiritualism, etc), and deeper discussion. So big names, no real focus on Jesus, structure, and encouraging discussion. On top of that they have marching and calisthenics—bodily gracefulness, which apparently even spirit children go in for—closing with a hymn and benediction.[39]

---

[39]   Bene = good; diction = speech. A benediction is speaking goodwill to folk to bless them, often as parting words. Instead of looking at the speaker speaking to them, Christians often close their eyes as if it's prayer.

Besides training up children to be good Spiritualists, Lyceums also encourage children to reach other children, and the other children to 'evangelise' their parents. Gasson added exhortation, even encouraging Christian children to receive spirit-baptism: he spoke of baptism in the Holy *Ghost*—old wording but quite common in those days.

In the sixties, fresh into Pentecostalism, I was asked by my high school classmates if I believed in ghosts. I said 'no'. I was then told that since I believed in the Holy Ghost, I believed in ghosts: a semi-logical argument at best—jumping from one ghost to many! Actually, other than in singing archaic songs, I don't think I used that term anyway, though I knew that some did. Most Christians nowadays speak rather of the Holy Spirit. *Ghost* used to be a medieval term for what nowadays we simply call, *spirit*.[40]

Gasson hoped youngsters would deeply encounter—called *immersion*, or *baptism*—the spirit, linking them to a supernatural flow and, like the primitive church, speaking from their spirits language they didn't understand but which enriched spiritually (1 Cor.14:18,4; Ac.11:16). He also took the line that children born to

---

[40]   Eg, for Mt.28:19 the Latin was *Spiritus Sancti*, but in the West Saxon of 990 it was *halgan gastes*, and *Hooli Goost* by the time of Wycliffe. *Ghost* was perhaps a bit too infected with false thinking even then. The KJV is a bit of mishmash on this: eg Jude 19 rendered the Greek word πνευμα/*pneuma* as 'spirit' in *Jude* 19, but 'ghost' in the next verse, being prefixed by 'holy'.

Christians are not born as Christians, but sometimes become Christians through Sunday School (G79).

On this last point I fully agree. Clearly a number of ideas have set in about how children can become Christians. Let's look at one of those ideas in a little depth. Decades ago, I was in a church leadership meeting where the lead pastor threw out that he believed that any child born of at least one Christian parent, was born with a ticket to heaven, and added that some might think that that was heresy.

I immediately said, "I do", to smiles all round. But how did his idea arise? I think it's like this: denomination B rejects something popular in denomination A, and then produces a variation of its disagreement. For instance, many Evangelicals, scotching the Roman Catholic idea of a rite of infant 'baptism' and carried over into Anglicanism, produce infant 'dedication' to cater for parents who might otherwise fear that their children were missing out on something vital.[41]

And likewise, some who don't believe that priestly water makes their children Christians, believe that parental faith rewards their children with free tickets to heaven, even if believing—in some Anglican way— that the ticket requires *confirmation* once the children reach a certain mental age of accountability, and

---

[41] I have no problem with *parent* dedication, where parents are publicly prayed for to be good parents. I recall being at one such dedication service led by Mr Michael Flowers, an A&E consultant from the Leeds General Infirmary. A very gracious, tender, and wise, man.

stamp the idea with the Evangelical *nihil obstat*. Why children born without a Christian parent don't get the ticket, tends to be a bit fuzzy.[42] The idea usually claims Pauline authority. Let's look at this.

For marriage and divorce in Paul's time, men usually had more so-called *rights*, and sometimes women weren't allowed to divorce. Of course, the NT neither teaches divorce as a willy-nilly 'right', nor unfairly treats the sexes *un*equally.

Now on the unequal theme, Paul neither rejected nor recommended mixed-faith marriages (1 Cor.7:39—why risk spiritual conflict?).[43] But he said that though mixed-faith marriages as such weren't sinful, they were spiritually risky. On the plus side, marriage to a nonbeliever could be spiritually positive, since the nonbeliever's closeness to the believer 'sanctified' him/her and any children they had, in some limited way (14). The Greek is ἅγιος/*hagios*, is usually put as 'sanctified', 'holy', or 'towards God'. Salvation?

Here it simply means that non-Christian spouses/children have a privileged closeness to the gospel through their spouse/parent. But that it gives them

---

[42]   If egalitarian Christians, unhappy with the "it's not who you know but who knows you", line, say that what one gets all should get, so free infant tickets for all, do they thus downrate or even dismiss the advantage of having a Christian parent?

[43]   Incidentally, Paul's position cuts across Spiritualism's idea of Twin Souls, of divorcing a mismatched soul to marry the right one, a romantic doctrine held by many. Paul was more for 'like it or lump it', and problem solving by internal management, not severance.

ultimate salvation, any guarantee of such, or even preferential treatment after death whatsoever, is simply a myth (1 Cor.7:16 applies the same way to offspring as to spouses). By not seeing that Paul's talk about children applies equally to spouses, some have fallen into the fallacy that if a parent has Christ, their children must have ultimate life.[44]

Well, where there's life, there's hope, so 'keep on praying' is good advice, but the desired result isn't biblically promised: living the witness is more biblical, and here to hope is more biblical than to believe. So, although God might give a spouse/parent such assurance, Paul did not. But other things being equal, having a Christian as spouse/parent puts their spouse/children in a better position to receive Christ. Ac.16:31 was either a specific prophecy about the jailer's family who would also hear the gospel, or given to assure the jailer—probably a believer in Mithraism, a military religion that taught that salvation was for men only—that salvation was also for women and children who could welcome Christ and be saved.

Likewise, though Ethnic Israel was *sanctified*—especially close to God—not all took advantage of this closeness to get to know him personally (eg Mt.8:11-2; Jhn.8:44-5). Paul said both that marriage to a

---

[44]   I use two contrasting terms for eternal life, namely *immediate* life (the steak on the plate while you wait), and *ultimate* life (the pie in the sky once you die), both aspects of spiritual salvation. The ultimate belongs to consummated eschatology, the former to realised eschatology.

nonbeliever bestowed added blessing on them, and that that blessing lacked guaranteed take-up: not all nonbelievers will open their family treasure chest. To sum up, properly reading Paul here shows that the key word (sanctified/holy) doesn't mean a heavenly ticket, and that what Paul applied to [unbelieving] children, he equally applied to unbelieving spouses.[45]

---

[45] The relevant passage is 1 Cor.7:12-6. Comparative grades: CEV (A+); NCV (B+); NABRE/NIV (C+); CEB (C-); ERV/LEB/NRSV (D); NKJV/NLT (D-).

Paul didn't guarantee that refusing to divorce, would help the other party. Nor was his point the well-being of any children, who statistically are harmed by divorce, especially if fault-free divorce becomes a role model inclining them against marriage. His was simply a preliminary understanding of the admissibility and advisability of divorce in that given situation. Christians would have to take it from there, possibly trying marriage counselling, yet in some cases speeding up their divorce—soonest mended.

Chapter 6

<u>Making Mediums</u>

An in-house course is used to mature new converts.[46] Spiritualism has Developing Circles, groups of people who are developing, maturing, within its vision, and can meet in private homes. 'Circle' indicates that idea that they gather around a table, of whatever shape. Somehow, 'Developing Square/Rectangle' just doesn't sound right. Experienced mediums are usually in charge, especially since 'mischievous', or even 'evil' spirits—said to be Earth-bound spirits of people who have unexpectedly died and don't quite realise or wish to realise where they are or what they are—might otherwise cause chaos and confusion.

Séances look to get the lighting just right for ambience. Red or blue aids restfulness, but normal lighting can work: candles in the dark aren't needed. Meetings might last a couple of hours, with nonintrusive

---

[46]   Incidentally, some churches likewise run maturation courses, but sadly many do not. Even so, regular church attendance, especially with participation, should pan out in maturation, and churches that seek to get folk involved, rather than being satisfied with 'pew fillers', can do the most good.

---

background music (while the 'sitters' focus on 'higher things'), relaxing (but not crossing their legs), possibly all joining hands (for an even distribution of power), and self-awareness dissolving away (a bit like self–hypnosis) so that the spirits might access minds: any thought is deemed likely to be from the 'spirit world'. Coming back to life, so to speak, each sitter will be asked what thoughts filled their minds.

Such individual feedback happens in charismatic churches—the first thing is to work out which side of the biblical divide you are, then ideally have your feedback assessed by mature Christians (1 Cor.14:29). At its high water mark, the Quakers/Shakers also had times when they happily met the first criterion: feedback was a big feature in the congregation, but perhaps uncritically assessed.[47] Many have moved in Christian circles from what is disparagingly called the one-man-band model, to a body-ministry[48] model, meaning a switchover from just some member of 'clergy' at the front running the whole show, to potentially each member of the 'laity' playing an active

---

[47]   So far as I can see, few if any of the Quakers nowadays would pass the first criterion, and feedback is on a pantheistic or panentheistic sub-Christian level: George Fox would weep.

[48]   Or *Body Building*: "the body...building up itself in love by the proper working of each individual part" (HCSB: Eph.4:16), using a human body to illustrate any local church, its people being its organic parts. Somewhat Orwellian, sometimes all are equal (under the shepherd), but some as under-shepherds are more equal than others.

---

part throughout meetings, under general submission to leadership.

In my experience, things more often stay with leadership than stray to 'laity', and such fits the image of shepherd/flock. Even with a 'body' illustration, a brain normally coordinates the organic whole.

Writing as a heavyweight Roman Catholic theologian, Hans Küng spoke radically in his book on ecclesiology, *The Church*. Hoping to devolve power from the top, he asked if there might be "a way back, which would also be a way forward, from this primacy of dominion to the old primacy of service and ministry" (Küng 1986:469).[49] I don't think that he minded the word *priest* having a subordinate ecclesiastical meaning, so long as that didn't undermine its broader pre-Eusebian meaning.

He said that it "is important that the positive significance of the priesthood of all believers be realised.... [Every Christian of either gender and any age, is able to have] direct access to God, [make] spiritual sacrifices...in a spirit of love and self-giving...preach the word and administer baptism, the Lord's Supper and the forgiveness of sins [having come into] the mediating work of the one and only mediator" (Küng 1986:372,381).

He begged Protestants to properly practice what they preached, namely the priesthood-of-all-believers. He stressed that 'laity' comes from λαος/*laos* (*people*) and leaders were part of God's people, while *clergy* comes from κληρος/*klēros* (*heritage*, the group of folk being

---

49   Küng said that the only way back from the wrong road and then forward on the right, was through a renunciation of papal power in favour of papal service.

~

guarded: 1 Pt.5:2-3): those led were the clergy, and their elders/*presbuteroi*—not 'priests'—would lead them. Terms swapped meanings, and 'clergy' came to stand for an educated (clerical) leadership, as distinct from an uneducated laity, and uneducated leadership—often the working class leading the working class, was edged out in favour of greater academics for 'clergy'.

As a Spiritualist group leader, Gasson generally had to deal with many figments of the imagination, for it is a medium's part to teach students to reach beyond imagination and to discriminate between 'evil' and 'good' spirits. It is reckoned that the sooner a student can see folly, the sooner they will see wisdom. Learning through failure, they who do not fail do not learn. Mediums feedback their own visions of the sittings, how they perceived the students, and describe the budding students' 'spirit guides'. And horses for courses, mediums can have more than one spirit guide.

In his very first sitting, Gasson had gone into deep trance and been controlled by a spirit guide which claimed to have died over 600 years ago as an African Witch Doctor, and claimed to now be his protective doorkeeper, keeping out evil spirits. Another sitter happened to know the African language of the guide, and enjoyed a friendly chat, interpreting into English, though I presume that the guide was at least bilingual. This guide worked healings and other phenomena, but in conjunction with another resident guide, 'direct voice' and 'materialisation' were produced while Gasson was in deep trance and unaware as to what was going on. When messiah led Gasson to oppose

Spiritualism, his then-doorkeeper, once friendly and familiar, turned from fascinating to frightening.[50]

Students are introduced to an encounter that parodies spirit-baptism.[51] Gasson repeated the point that there is clear blue water between the baptism in *one* spirit, and baptisms into/by *many* spirits, *spirits*-baptism, we may say. He spoke of having experienced both. Guide

---

[50]   One might think of *The Matrix*, where Neo was safe from the Matrix while he was controlled by it, but unsafe from it once he awoke to what it was.

[51]   1 Cor.12:13. There are genuine translation options here, and interpretation kicks in. I take εν/*en* as locative: baptised *in* one spirit. Here the unity (whether ethnic Jews or not; whether socially free or slaves), rather than God the spirit's holiness, is highlighted in this context. Next, I take εις/*eis* in its sense of 'relating to' (relative to being one body). [Wycliffe took it to mean 'into' (in to one body), while Tyndale took it to mean 'in order to' (to make one body). Bishops, and Douay Rheims, returned to Wycliffe.]

I hold that spirit-baptism is subsequent to conversion (and it can predate (Ac.10:47) or postdate (Ac.8:16) *water-baptism*, both baptisms being post-conversional). Combining points by Gordon Fee (on the epexegetical use of και/*kai*) & D A Carson (on ποτιζειν/*potizein*: to drench vs to drink—incidentally in the one-off/emphatic aorist tense, as is water-baptism), I take that next part to have been Paul repeating himself: that is, his audience had all been once for always drenched relative to one spirit, though I still like Wycliffe's "ben fillid with drink", even if drinking in the spirit lacks biblical precedent as an illustration: on this see David Garland's: *1 Corinthians* (BECNT), 2015, loc. 13569/28028.

spirits more or less always watch over their mediums (hence 'familiar'), and are the first to be triggered whenever their medium seeks to be controlled. The guides allow other spirits to work through their medium, and to directly or indirectly pass on data. Guide control can be lite (mental) or trance (usually physical). If lite, the medium's usual voice and consciousness are active, though words and mind are subordinate to the guide's.

But at trance level, the medium's breathing becomes deeper, then stops for a second or so, at which point some suggest that the medium's spirit leaves to make way for their guide—it is as if they later 'return' from a time of vague brightness.[52] Their body becomes as cold as death, and the voice is distinct according to the guide spirit. Sitters can feel a cool breeze from the guide, or warmth if it is a healing guide.

Trance itself has two levels, lite and deep. The latter is for more intense physical mediumship, and leaves mediums completely exhausted to the point of post-traumatic trembling. It's suggested that that is the price paid for allowing the guide to utilise bodily energy to produce physical phenomena—the greater the tax, the greater the payment.

Guide 'entrance/egress' can be hazardous. If the sitters cause disturbance, the medium's body can suffer the consequences—it can be fatal. During deep trance OOBE, the medium's spirit is said to travel through

---

[52]   Gasson neither concluded that a theorised OOBE was factual nor false, but for convenience spoke in terms of it being factual, a convenience I follow.

realms of light, but Gasson said that he travelled through realms of darkness during his last trance, the spirits trying to prevent his return to his body—ie, attempted murder. An alternative explanation could be that the sitters had caused some disturbance, which by his own reckoning could lead to a medium's spirit dying in transit. However, he spoke of some third-party suddenly stepping in to bring him home.

He did not say whether he questioned the sitters afterwards, however, his stated belief is probably correct, for a pure coincidence between his bad experience and his good entertaining of messianic ideas, would have been quite remarkable. Besides, he mentioned how after this last séance, the spirits tried to force him into a trance state, presumably with no good intended.

Developing Circle students will often see coloured lights, with each colour carrying its own meaning—eg healing, purity, love. Such lights are often seen when mediums are about to enter into a trance. Guides often claim to come from a different nation and language-group, and sometimes someone else in a trance will, by their guide, interpret into English (or whatever) what the unknown language means. Gasson dismissed any true links between this and the Day of Pentecost (Ac.2), drawing on his explanation that one is the demonic counterfeit of God's genuine article. The idea that Pentecost's 'tongues of fire' were Spiritualist spirit-lights, or that Pentecost's spirit was an incoming of spirits from high spheres, Gasson rubbished, underlining how Scripture speaks is such contexts of the one spirit, the Holy Spirit, the spirit of Yahweh.[53] He ridiculed the idea that the early Welsh revival had—and Pentecostal churches have—Spiritualistic phenomena without realising it: the counterfeit hides behind the genuine, and it's by their differences that we can tell them apart.

I agree with Gasson and M F Bovenizer, that Christianity should be demonstrable. But *pace* Gasson, I no longer cite from Mk.16:9-20 to prove biblical points.[54] I suspect that if the church played her part, we would see more demonstration of the spirit's power. While miracles are not part of the 'full gospel', they can be part of preaching the gospel fully (Rm.15:19).

---

[53] Incidentally in quoting Jg.6:34, Gasson's text has "Spirit of the Lord". I agree that it was neither about any old spirit nor multiple spirits, but he, his editor, or both, showed carelessness by not following Tyndale (and the KJV) in putting [LORD]. LORD—not Lord—was Tyndale's code for God's name, *Yahweh*. Such careless writing leads to (and from) careless theology, to undermining the church, and so to undermining society.

[54] Some argue that Mk.16:9-20 was by Mark (so canonical), so why drop it? Prof. F F Bruce noted that discoveries have shown that it was not by Mark (so noncanonical), so why keep it? Does Mk.16:12-3 really fit with Lk.24:33-5? The ancient versions either 1# end with v8, 2# follow v8 by a short ending, or 3# follow v8 by a long ending: the long ending (3#) has better claim to be early (perhaps early C2), than the short ending (2#). Most hold that Mark either A# ended his Gospel with γαρ/*gar* (for...) for dramatic effect (a unique ending but possible), or B# that his ending has been lost.

I suspect that in turn God would play things less demonstrably than some of us wish, but more than some of us wish. But that more counterfeit money swims around than genuine money, neither make the counterfeit genuine, not switches the relationship.

Chapter 7

Skyping Spirits

Gasson went into some depth about what's called clairvoyance and clairaudience, and deemed by Spiritualists to be one natural gift of two sides. Some suggest that such is what Paul spoke about regarding the spiritual ability to distinguish between spirits (1 Cor.12:10's διακρισεις πνευματων/*diakriseis pneumatōn*).[55]

---

[55]   Paul chucked in a few then familiar abilities under then common names. Truth divorced from experience must always dwell in the realm of doubt. With losing the common abilities through long divorce, we have lost that common language of spiritual manifestations, though for the most part have been able to rebuild it. But to some limited extent, 1 Cor.12:10 is open for grabs.

Gasson's interpretation was probably correct, namely God enabling us to sometimes spot the origins behind non-natural phenomena, including visions: in practice this might be like a gut feeling upon hearing of this or that vision, for they can be triggered by the deific, by the demonic, or by the human. Wayne Grudem noted how, for instance, epilepsy could be triggered by subnatural (Mt.17:14-8) or natural (Mt.4:24) causes (*Systematic Theology*, 1994:425). Psychiatrist John White (in *Masks of Melancholy*) confessed that in some

---

That was rejected by Gasson, who had lived both sides of the fence. For one thing its *modus operandi* was different, in that the deific manifestation gently imparts revelation, leaving the mental faculties untouched and undisturbed, unlike the demon control for subnatural sight and sound. The audience around Mount Sinai were not in a passive mode, nor were the disciples on the Mount of Transfiguration—the appearances hit them out of the blue![56] Nor did Paul clearly extend this spiritual ability/manifestation to sight & sound.

Non-Spiritualists sometimes confuse clairvoyance and clairaudience, with mind reading and character reading—discerning someone's faults and failings. Clairvoyance is actually seeing spirits; clairaudience is actually hearing spirits. As for the content of clairaudience, it is basically a heap of passable stuff with darkness smuggled in, apples with dark worms and not much juice in the apples. The spirits can happily talk about messiah's blood and quote Jesus, but only without God's power behind their words. Bibles and séances seem to walk happily hand in hand.

---

cases he had found it difficult to diagnose between demonic and natural causes.

[56] Probably at Mount Meron (rather than Tabor or Hermon), about a seven-hour walk from Capernaum. The name form Elias (G93) basically follows the Greek/Latin. One of the earliest scholars to switch over, John Wesley, followed the Hebrew form, Elijah (a.k.a. Eliyah), which is standard nowadays.

Gasson took to task a particular superstition of some Christians.[57] Too often Christians he met seemed to think that Christian signs and speech worked like magic—which is to misunderstand Christian signs and speech. For instance, talk of Jesus' blood biblically means his redemptive death, but some Christians throw the term around willy-nilly. They might think that their house is safe from burglars and floods because it's 'under the blood'—in their dreams! Gasson held that only our sins are under the blood, that is, covered by Christ's death (Rm.4:7), and that by its power (not its covering) we can win spiritual battles. But believing that we should ask God to cover our meetings by Christ's blood, is begging for spiritual blindness. He reckoned that if our core ideas are right, then our extended ideas are more likely to be right, and best if we also walk in line with the Holy Spirit. I suspect that he had had some heated discussions with fellow Christians on this topic.

Mediums can usually see and hear spirits without needing special lighting—a bus, a public park in daylight, whatever. As said, it's deemed a natural ability, a sensitising of the mind to see and hear human spirits no longer living in physical bodies. Some become very sensitive to such spirits. Trance state isn't needed. Gasson told a funny story of a public meeting where a 'sign and symbol' medium—one who is

---

[57] Superstition is a thing I knock in my book, *Vampire Count*: sorry Bram Stoker, but the flash of a cross doesn't make vamps cringe in fear, and Dracula could happily don a crucifix.

unusually a bit fuzzy in clairvoyance and clairaudience —addressed a woman in the audience, whom she said had a spirit mustard tin hovering over her head. It was a 'No I haven't/Yes you have' dingdong, but at last the woman confessed that her surname was Coleman, and satisfied that its job was done, the mustard tin spirit sailed off into the spirit world.

Gasson added that Christians should know that it's *impossible* for the deceased to return to us, whatever the fun factor (G98). Since later he accepted that Yahweh can send them back (G143), perhaps he should have nuanced his wording: *impossible* perhaps for us to summon them, *or* for them to initiate, but not *for Yahweh* to send them (Mk.10:27).[58]

Mediums seek to make genuine connections between individual spirits and sitters, before passing on any message from spirit to sitter. At the level of clairvoyance, usually only the medium sees the spirit, and the medium seeks to ensure that the spirit is who it claims to be, since bad spirits can cause confusion. Self-identity claims are considered proven if the spirit easily answers the questions correctly, including intimate details which only the deceased and the sitter are presumed to have known. Sometimes the spirit knows something so private that not even the sitter knows it until they check it out. All this can seem a pretty conclusive identity test.

---

[58]   This text is abused by overweight. God cannot do the in-itself, intrinsic, impossible, such as creating a weight he cannot lift.

A suspicious mind might suggest that sometimes sitters are in on the trick—and they probably are within fake Spiritualism, the counterfeit of the counterfeit. But some genuine sitters get hooked because the spirit knew some hidden family detail that seemingly only the deceased could have known. However, all such 'proof' counts for nothing, if the spirits are shadow spirits who shadowed the human beings they subsequently impersonate, since the shadow could know what the deceased knew.

Gasson suggested a combination of shadow information plus mind-reading/telepathy. Shadowing is perhaps implied by spirits who claim to guide people before death—all guides are shadows, though not all shadows are guides! Mind-reading is presumed by the spirits at times saying that when they saw such and such a sitter at such and such a time, the sitter was *thinking* such and such. Spirits can make minor slips, such as saying that they saw someone's gold watch, when in fact it was a silver watch—but human observers can make the same minor slips, and the spirits do not claim omniscience.

Gasson suggested a populous and powerful global intelligence network of demons, perhaps with some kind of psychic databasing, although the spirits summoned to any given séance might simply be the particular ones who had shadowed the humans they claimed to be. Let humanity beware and take hope.

Chapter 8

Feelings in the Mind

Mental mediumship includes psychometry. The idea is that given an item touched by someone now dead or distant, data can be drawn from their 'etheric vibrations'. Mediums consider this low-tech stuff, but good for business. Since being studious gains better results, mediums are encouraged to perfect their skills. Usually, any private and confidential data revealed by spirits will be kept between the medium and the enquirer, sparing blushes, though obviously some mediums will be more tactful than others, according to personality types and maturity.

Psychometry, effective bait to catch anxious parents during WW2, was also used to find missing persons. Results are rather mixed. Sometimes it has reported that that someone hasn't been killed, when in fact they have. But fish can be caught whether using real or false bait, and once caught can be in the bag. During WW2 Gasson, psychometrising an item, reported the soldier to be a POW. The father disagreed—he had a telegram officially reporting his son as killed in action. Gasson's guide said that its own report would be verified within three days—and it was. Spirits one; War Office minus one—the War Office had made a clerical error. Did the demon know that, cause that, sort that? Who is to say.

Gasson held psychometry to be the demonic counterfeit to the spiritual manifestations of words of knowledge/wisdom (1 Cor.12:8). Paul's biblical meaning would approximate to bits of data coming from God to help someone out (knowledge), or him suggesting a way forward, a solution that suddenly comes out of the blue as the perfect solution (wisdom)—both have a 'wow' factor, manifestations of God's spirit.

Jesus was not a medium,[59] but some say that Jhn.4 records him psychometrising the water bucket which the woman had touched. That's reading rather a lot into a text that doesn't bother to say whether Jesus even got his drink, let alone—had he done so—think it important enough (not even as a teaching exercise for budding mediums?) to mention the bucket, though of major importance in psychometry.

Their argument is, If you can't prove he didn't, we can assume that he did. They hold that he must have done things their way, and that therefore he surely had done things their way. Thus they assume their conclusion— circular reasoning. In claiming to see invisible fern seed far away, they overlook the visible elephant under their very noses, the message that Jesus gave the woman of the epochal dawn of messianism, opening true worship of the father (Jhn.4:23-9).

---

[59] Medium, no; mediator, yes. He was mediator of a new covenant, created by his voluntary death (1 Tm.2:5; Heb.9:15).

Chapter 9

Battered Bodies

Gasson spoke of what is commonly called 'divine healing' by believers, 'faith healing' by sceptics, and 'deific healing' by me. In Spiritualist circles (as in Christian) physical blindness, deafness, lameness, can all be healed. But at what spiritual cost to those healed? What if you've got to pay the piper? What if Abba's song applies, namely that the Angel Eyes that speak of paradise, are hell disguised, leading to tragic loss? What if helping your body, harms your soul?

The Bible is full of healing miracles, and Paul spoke of Christians having authority and power under deity to heal (eg 1 Cor.12:9).[60] Spiritualists happily claim to side with Paul here, and sincerely put themselves out to the point of physical exhaustion, just to see others healed. Prayerfully placing hands on someone has biblical backing, eg Ac.28:8, but that does not mean that Spiritualists copying that practice have biblical power.

---

[60]   The Greek, χαρισματα ιαματων/*charismata iamatōn*, seems to me to emphasise both the graciousness (*charis*) of this manifestation of the spirit, and branches of healing (*mata* being a plural form).

Spiritualists hold that healing mediums have healing hands, and that fellow believers can add power to those hands by the likes of 'love rays'.

For allowing Satan to claim the healing high ground, Gasson scathingly castigated the church. I suspect that he was somewhat OTT here, and certainly so if he believed that everyone is supposed to be physically healed by God in the here and now.[61] That said, many who could be somatically healed aren't, because the church lacks in the belief that God deificly heals, or she is simply too afraid of failing. That he heals through doctors (and pray that their skills are honed) is fine. He can also heal through herbs and sleep—all ways within his natural provision for people to draw physical help from their surrounds and from each other. But preventing access to deific healing is rather like preventing access to the NHS. Neither the NHS nor God—for various reasons—will heal everyone who seeks treatment, but some will be healed.

Another Christian practice is lifted from Jas.5:14: "Are any of you sick? You should call for the elders of the church to come and pray over you, anointing you with oil in the name of the lord" (NLT). The early apostles had acted likewise (Mk.6:13). This in turn was lifted from a

---

[61]   Two texts sourced in Is.53:5, spring to mind. 1 Pt.2:24 drew out its higher spiritual healing side; Mt.8:17 drew out its lower physical healing side, subservient to the greater good, and particularly switched on as a sign to conversion (Lk.5:23). Physical healings might be 'in the atonement', but so are resurrection bodies: some healings must await the resurrection, whether needfully or not.

Sinaitic background, where oil symbolised a touch from God. "James' recommendation that regular church officers carry out the practice, would seem to imply its permanent validity in the church. On the other hand, the fact that anointing a sick person is mentioned only here in the NT letters, and that many healings were accomplished without anointing [oil], shows that the practice is not a necessary accompaniment to the prayer for healing" (Douglas J Moo's *James* (TNTC), 1990:179). [62] Another procedure, even less common in churches, is a word of command (Ac.14:10). [63]

All these methods can be used in private home circles by a healing medium, often accompanied by soft music or singing, and under lite control (for easy illnesses) or trance (for deeper illnesses). For really serious problems, a patient might require hypnosis to endure related pain. [64] Sitters can focus on wishing healing for those

---

[62]   In choosing between χριω/*chriō* and αλειφω/*aleiphō*, James probably plumped for the latter because whereas in Christian talk the former emphasised metaphysical, leadership anointing, the latter emphasised physical anointing yet could, like the former, speak of spiritually connecting to God (Moo 1990:180), and with the similar word remind them that as Chri-stians (from *chri-ō*) they were metaphysically anointed (set aside) unto God. *Aleiphō* sometimes carries the idea of rubbing oil.

[63]   My *Prayer's Gone Global*, covers this in some depth.

[64]   Christians divide over the issue of hypnosis. Some say that hypnotists cannot force the hypnotised to do anything they reject at core level, and that it no more opens them up to demonisation than does sleep. However, downloading a file without either the filter of a firewall or of anti-virus software, is dangerous, since

named, and rightly feel that they are playing their part. They also offer 'absent healing', extending physical healing to people not physically present.[65]

Healing can also extend to animals—the nonhuman, not the inhuman sort, just to be clear. John Wesley successfully prayed for his horse to be healed, but then that was as needful as praying for your conked car to start when you're heading off to evangelism—though the horsepower is somewhat more. Nevertheless, Gasson added that God sometimes seems to heal beloved pets we pray for—and why not? From a Spiritualist perspective, of course, the spirits of pets can seem to have just as much entitlement to mediumistic help as human spirits.

After his conversion, Gasson met a woman who had been cured of physical blindness by a medium and refused to see—even though he spoke as someone who had journeyed through Spiritualism into Christianity—that the good work had been done by a bad source, and that the bad source did it for bad ends. He again referred to Spiritualism as a cult (G115)—I

---

an uncritically accepted file might smuggle in a bad payload. We should guard what comes into our minds and maximise self-control, but arguably, accompanied by family or friend, someone trained both in hypnosis and godly counselling could, like gene therapy, aid good mental therapy by implanting useful code in safe mode.

65   Gasson added that if Spiritualist home groups can engage in false healing prayer, shouldn't Christians meet in home groups and engage in true healing prayer? Why be shown up by the devil? Why should the devil have all the good music?

---

suggest that the term *occultus* (as a branch of the occult) could be used as a better noun. I think that Spiritualism is substantially unlike our general idea of cults, namely some kind of system that's substantially deviant from the norm and that's into people-control (a.k.a. 'heavy shepherding'). Deemed an occultus (like witchcraft), the subnatural practice would be the headline flag, rather than its heterodox belief.

To highlight the ideal, he quoted the *Psychic News*. It commended the healing abilities of an *Assemblies of God* pastor, but asked, why should the AoG condemn Spiritualism, when Spiritualism didn't condemn the AoG? Like Hinduism, Spiritualism seems happy to accept others and to be accepted as a valid (and best) way among many. Gasson highlighted that there is only one road to true (αληθινος/*alēthinos*) worship of God the father (Jhn.14:6),[66] and that Spiritualism is not it. Rather, he maintained that there are many roads to perdition, and that Spiritualism is one of them, even though it be paved with good intentions.

---

[66]   Inexclusivism holds that the exclusive way to God as an individual's heavenly father, is through Jesus; other ways can inclusively lead to God as God.

Chapter 10

Beached Whales

"But if I use the power of God's spirit to force out demons, then the kingdom of God has come to you" (NCV: Mt.12:28). So, far from the idea that he worked miracles by his own deificity, this implies that he worked them by reliance on God's spirit—a pattern for us. Too easily we escape doing stuff that Jesus did, because, we say, he did them by his deificity and we're not deific.

It's true we're not, and it's true that Jesus lived and operated as a fully human being, the New Adam, not as deity. Paul also went in for casting out evil spirits. But as an early Christian, Paul was not the only show casting out demons. He must have had outstanding results, but trying his method required a connection to messiah and the spirit, not some magic formula, as sons of an ethno-Jewish priest named Sceva soon discovered to their cost (Ac.19:13-5).[67] So, do *Christian*

---

[67]   This is not to say that non-Christian exorcists might not have some authority from God and truly cast out demons. Mk.9:38 (a proto-Christian believer?) and Mt.12:27 (Sinai-believers), seem to me to countenance such a service under Sinai, and perhaps, like prayer,

---

Spiritualists not operate this Christian duty of care? Are they not in messiah? Do they not tap into Yahweh's spirit?

Some claim to do so, but Gasson basically said that theirs was a very different sort of show, a sideshow by Satan's spirits, not expulsion of them by God's spirit. He put emphasis on Jesus' 'name', any lesser authority being powerless. Is any lesser authority powerless? Maybe, but I'm not so sure, largely on the basis that Yeshua seems to me to have validated exorcisms done under Sinai—hardly under his 'name'—but also on the belief that people who know nothing of messiah could still be godly and still have God's help against the demonic. I insist merely that it is a hunch on my part.

As to 'my name', Gasson was on shaky ground when he cited the longer ending to *Mark*, but the NT does show that Jesus' 'name' generally carried the ideas of those within his community having his general authority when being under his general authority/will (living as he generally would if in their shoes), and having his specific authority/will when being under his specific authority/will (acting as he would do in their given situations). In my first 'preach' as a Mattersey Hall[68] student, 'on the block' I opined that Paul at Lystra had been mistaken not to mention the name *Jesus* (Ac.14:10), a mistake he remedied at Philippi (Ac.16:18). The brashness of my youth, perhaps? Now older even

---

pagan people also had enough grace from God to perhaps overcome the demonic now and again.

[68] From 1973 to 2021, it was the British AoG's theological college, in Nottinghamshire.

---

if not wiser, I maintain my position that while naming Jesus as our authority is right, throwing his name at situations can be treating his name as a magic formula, treating it superstitiously. At Lystra, deific healing happened without mentioning the name Jesus: the problem was the crowd thinking that the channels were the source.

Gasson also cited the sons of Sceva (Ac.19:15), although the Greek is better brought out by the NIV: "...the evil spirit answered them, 'Jesus I know, and Paul I know about, but who are you?'" It would not release its victim to folk flying under false colours who lacked the authority to evict it, and who were at best presuming that Yeshua was a prophet under Sinai.[69] But what they attempted was very different from Spiritualists who switch to talk about Rescue Work. In short, they consider the troubling spirit to be in trouble and require rescuing as an act of kindness, not as an enemy but as a friend, to help them swim off from mortal shores into the spirit sea where they belong. Spiritualism posits a spirit world, consisting of lower and higher spheres/planes/levels, with normal progress for all from lower to higher. Someone sinful in mortal life will pay for their sins by the sphere in which they find themselves in immediately after

---

[69] I picture an unauthorised tenant, but along with the term 'possession', perhaps we should not too strongly focus on the idea of *indwelling*, with its concomitant questions as to the manner of indwelling. I have heard debates about whether it's the physical body that's indwelt, or whether it's the 'soul', or whether it's the 'spirit'. *Demonisation* is perhaps the most neutral term.

death—it will serve them right and teach repentance. Centuries might pass until they realise their sinfulness, repent, and move higher, presumably their inner change simply evolves them up the ladder.

Some hold that this postmortem stage has included reincarnation, that is, going through at least one other human body to become a better person, purging away sin. They would say that an Einstein would be an 'old soul', a genius after many reincarnations; an invalid would have chosen invalidity to pay for sins of a previous life. A still-born baby would simply have needed a final brief innings to be fit for the spirit world. Some extend reincarnation to a whole system of spirit evolution from single-cell life upto and through human life, before becoming a ball of light.

The idea is that some bad spirits don't repent, so neither ascend higher as spirits, nor return to Earth reincarnated—they merely return to/stay on Earth as nonmaterial spirits, disturbing themselves and others. These 'earthbound spirits' need rescuing from their evil ways. Mediums who are said to be 'old souls', seem best placed to sort out earthbound fallen spirits, since they can best explain to the fallen what they are, where they should go, and how.

Rescue Work can involve friendly persuasion—but not all fallen spirits like to be messed with. Home Circles are the frequent venue for the teamwork usually required to correct the truculence of the fallen. Dim light can aid concentration. Protection by the higher spirit world from the lower spirit world, can be prayed for. The Circle seeks to think like a magnet, attracting errant spirits to come to be rescued. The Rescue

Medium allows a fallen spirit to control their body, while the team tries to teach the fallen spirit. Usually there's a fight: the medium's body can get thrown about; they can use vile language; objects can get thrown at the team—best to remove furniture—and murders have been attempted. There are suggested ways to hold a medium's body to prevent the fallen spirit from simply escaping before being taught in the way it should go. Mediums can seem stronger than they usually are—to some extent anyone can seem so if their pain sensors are switched off.

The rescue crew are vilified by fallen spirits as children of light, tormentors of the fallen. If the bad spirit gets too stroppy, a medium will ask their guide spirit to take over and talk to the fallen. Success usually comes, when the bad spirit calms down and learns its lessons. Well, if a fisherman always loses the fish, they'll give up fishing: Gasson said that here it is the fishers not the fish, that are in fact being caught by the 'bait', conned by clever demons.

Usually, the fallen then confess their sins, seek forgiveness, and leave with the guides to higher spheres. Some of the fallen seem to be merely confused spirits, not realising that they have died or that they are in the 'wrong body' of the medium! It's as if one minute it felt pain (for example being run over), and the next it's surrounded by strangers in a dim room, wondering what on Earth is going on. It might seem to feel embarrassed at having troubled anybody.

Gasson related how one such spirit, hosted by himself for its rescue, was told that it was to ascend higher and to work for the good of mankind. Apparently, it got into a huff at the idea of work, saying that it had never done a day's work in its life and didn't mean to begin now—do demons have a sense of humour? Gasson called all such goings on, play acting on the side of both the 'fallen' and the 'guides'.

Haunted Houses is a fun game. At one old Hampstead house, knocks and bangs in the nights disrupted sleep; items got moved around by unseen 'hands'; whatever could get filled with water, got filled with water. A medium was asked to lay the ghost. The first demon was seemingly unhappy at having attracted evil spirits to help him sort out his old enemy—the house owner. This spirit had apparently come back from the spirit world for a little bit of revenge, but uninvited a heavy mob had gatecrashed the party—all too much for this poor spirit, who begged to be rescued from the mess it had created. After it was sorted and sent packing, the nastier spirits had to be sorted. One at a time they were seemingly led to repentance and deliverance, leaving the happy owners with the house all to themselves.

Spiritualists say that Rescue Work is all about evil spirits being cast out, and that since a house torn apart by infighting will collapse (Mk.3:25), it cannot be the work of evil spirits casting out other evil spirits, and therefore must be the work of good spirits casting out evil spirits. While they're not daft enough to divide their own kingdom, they're clever enough to divide daft humanity, it seems.

For rescue mediumship is not *casting out* evil spirits at all, and the devil's house is united in impersonating human spirits, some playing good cop, some playing bad con, the latter giving up the fight before the Circle collapses, as if a fish wishing to be caught but not too easily. Then, said Gasson, both trot off together to laugh at the credulity of human nature that makes it possible for such a hoax to be played out. Biblically, exorcism is commanding nonhuman evil spirits (demons) to depart as defeated enemies, not trying to educate human spirits into departing as friends.

Chapter 11

Up Close and Personal

Mental mediumship allows sitters to hear words *via* a medium, and even to see facial reshapings that ID the guide spirits, even feeling a difference. For instance, if the medium is puny, a 'strong' spirit might exude a sense of largeness, although the medium's body retains its own size. Physical mediumship is another level, potentially one of touch.

Under trance, it seems that a substance is drawn from the medium, like a semi-luminescent thick mist creeping from their eyes, ears, nose, throat, or perhaps the stomach. [70] This *ectoplasm* becomes solid for

---

[70]   Perhaps the molecular substance is formed from the surrounding air by the spirits—somewhat as water vapour can condense on car windows on frosty nights—and by their design then flows forth from various parts of mediums' bodies. Thelodynamic control over atoms. Similarly, for postmortal life, where nature and spirit will be in perfect harmony, will we not, as spirits made perfect, summon atoms to clothe us in physical imperishability? For heaven for us will be where spirit and physicality truly belong inseparably, more like being centaurs than riding horses. Incidentally, Lewis scotched the fantasy that the molecules that composed

physical manifestations. Since sensitive to light, it is produced in the dark, although limited success has been achieved in lighter settings. Touching it is only safe under certain conditions, and with proper permissions. Call it shy, so to speak, but touch must be expected and gentle, lest still in semi-solid state it tries to retreat into the medium's body without first returning into its gaseous state. Liken that to someone unexpectedly inhaling freezing water instead of warm air, or to a heavy elastic band hitting an eye at speed. Hurt can cause the medium to scream in pain. Harm can cripple and blind the medium in severe cases.

Gasson was almost blinded in one such incident. Yet with permission, pieces have actually been cut off, showing it to be like something between a cheese muslin and fine linen. Police investigators have been known to grab it, be pulled towards the medium, and then charge the medium with fraud, on the assumption that the missing evidence was something like muslin. Unjustly condemned, one poor lady (though the evidence was missing) spent most of her jail time recovering in hospital.

The phenomena can be faked, and Spiritualists are among the first to pick up on fakes. Theatre Magicians can justifiably reproduce such phenomena through trickery, but then that is their trade. Gasson spoke of tests that made faking impossible. For instance, mediums can be thoroughly searched beforehand, or

our physicality in mortal life are eternally specific to us: molecules recycle in nature (C S Lewis' *Miracles*, 1947:179).

perform in swim gear, being bound or held while ectoplasm is formed. In physical séances there can be levitation of furniture and of people, even floating in and out of windows. Seemingly telekinesis can transport items undamaged through solid walls and doors. Musical instruments can be played without being touched. All very fascinating stuff. Gasson again raised the issue of counterfeiting, even to the extent that Spiritualists should not get away with being the only show in town, since the biblical charismata have never been withdrawn from service. Should Christians not show the world the real charismata from God?

Another phenomenon is *transfiguration*. At a low level it is common enough among mediums, and usually done in their own homes rather than in open meetings. In a dark room, a spotlight will be shone on the medium's face. Usually, the medium will enter trance state. Sitters will wait while a mist obscures the face, slowly forming another face—man, woman, or child—a face known to at least one sitter, but the face will be left to identify itself. The colour of the eyes will be just right, irrespective of the medium's eye colour. A succession of faces follow, each allowing their linked sitter to converse with them, and things can get quite emotional. Sitters can hear messages of forgiveness, while their *love rays* are thought to be fed into the medium, increasing their power.

There is also Direct Voice, generally within dark rooms. Such mediums can be called Trumpet Mediums, for they use at least one trumpet. Trumpets are painted with luminous paint. Trance Mediums will go into a trance for better results. Sitters are always cautioned, for ectoplasm will be at work, trumpets being connected to the medium by an ectoplasmic rod. Any trumpet used will float around, and a spirit, using ectoplasm for a voice box, will speak through it. To encourage such phenomena, sitters can sing to stimulate good vibrations, and when all is ready the room temperature drops, and the atmosphere become tense. Trumpets will whiz around the room, narrowly missing sitters. One trumpet might speak while another one sings. Each has its unique ID. Speech and singing will sound just like the voices of the departed, counterfeits to a tee. Trumpet séances can last well over an hour, before the tired old trumpets slowly return to their original positions.

Some say that when Jesus was baptised, the heavenly voice spoke through a trumpet (Mt.3:17). But where was the trumpet, the dark room, the singers to keep up the good vibrations? There is some very superficial thinking by Spiritualists here, in seeking to name and claim messianic alignment. No doubt Spiritualists wish to be what they wish Jesus to have been, and so manage to convince themselves on very superficial readings—what Freud called wish fulfilment.

Chapter 12

Some Body or Other

Mt.11:5 speaks of people coming back from death, and Mt.10:8 is probably a command given by Jesus to his then disciples to physically, not metaphysically, raise folk from death. In one incident, "as they came near the gate of a town, they saw people carrying out the body of a widow's only son. Many people from the town were walking along with her.... Then Jesus walked over to the coffin and touched it, and the bearers stopped. 'Young man,' he said, 'I tell you, get up'" (CEV/NLT: Lk.7:12,14— modified). To me this hardly looks like a medium summoning up a ghost in any sense or shape. It's like walking down a street on a bright summer's day, seeing a corpse on its way to be buried, stopping the hearse, reanimating the body, and the person taking a taxi back home, perhaps to die again in sixty years' time.

It's important to grasp that such interventions were strategic, that they were rare, that they affected only those recently deceased, that the reanimated would live to die again another day, and that—over and above messianic reanimations being rare forms of kindness—by God's spirit they hinted to the people that messiah had come, he who would bring about the ultimate resurrection. Before Yeshua died, the most remarkable reanimating was of Lazarus, having been dead for four days. Jewish leadership was so annoyed that it planned to kill off Lazarus (Jhn.11:43; 12:10).

In Spiritualist circles, *materialisation*—their way to raise folk from death—is well short of having people resume normal life on earth. Materialism merely means spirits taking on ectoplastic, tangible forms, matching the human appearance of those they impersonate. Ectoplastic bodies are not living and breathing somatic bodies.

Sometimes the medium will sit aloof from the sitters. Those who believe in prayer, will pray. The room is dark. The guide takes control, and reminds folk of the safety rules, the main one being not to touch without permission. Singing is lively to raise the vibration levels, and the semi-luminous ectoplasm seems to flow forth, slowly gaining human form, from feet upwards. Once complete, the body is able to walk to the person it wishes to talk with, and even to shake hands. Gasson recalled the chilling coldness of spirit 'hands', the hardness of 'bones' and 'knuckles'. One can even stroke spirit-cats, and the spirits even do birds, for those whose pets have gone the way of all flesh. A number of spirit-forms can be on the go at the same time, but the other sitters should keep singing—it's rude to stop unless spoken to. You can have spirit-water thrown at you for not singing—all good clean fun of course. Several ectoplastic bodies can be walking about, alongside trumpets that whizz around but avoid both spirit-bodies and sitters, being channels for unmaterialised spirits.

Gasson theorised that demons crave physical embodiment, and find that mediumistic ectoplasm gives them that for brief spaces of time. There is some evidence for this, specifically Mt.8:31/Mk.5:12/Lk.8:32.[71] However in this biblical incident it's unlikely that they wished to rehouse for their comfort. For Scripture neither teaches that those angels who fell into sin became disembodied, nor that they had ever required physical bodies for comfort. Moreover, these Gospels show that "the first thing the demons did was to precipitate the death of their new 'home'" (D A Carson's *Matthew* (EBC), 2010:430). I think it more likely that they hoped to trick Jesus into letting them damage his reputation in that area, and that seeing through their trick he played along, letting them work their evil because he could turn it for the greater good, outfoxing the outfoxers: see Gen.50:20.[72]

Gasson cited missionary stories about real demons dwelling in real idols, but we don't have to agree as to why they can seemingly indwell such. Is it for their comfort (so G141), or is it simply as convenient bases of operation, where they can best focus the faith and fear of the local human population, and thus control them?

---

[71]   Folklore about vampires drowning could have begun with confusing them with demons, plus not understanding that only the pigs, not their demonic guests, drowned to death. My *Vampire Count*, has Dracula swimming in the Danube for the sheer fun of it.

[72]   Though the herd owners lost a valuable asset, they gained a more valuable lesson as to Yeshua's authority, perhaps eventually becoming Christians: evils can be to glorify (ie point towards) God (Jhn.9:2-3).

I suspect that some demons might well have spoken through idols, even as they can through mediums.[73] At the end of the day Gasson could only theorise on this, and his Spiritualistic past did not give him any specialist insight here.

Gasson argued that the common trance-and-control state bought some happy home time for unhappy spirits, the idea being that the medium's spirit leaves an empty house for the demon spirit to relax in for an hour or so. I am a little puzzled here, for it seems to me that he made a case here for demons preferring nonmaterialisation to materialisation, and actually making it difficult for mediums to perfect the art—he mentioned one medium trying for 22 years before becoming a Trumpet Medium, although adding that it doesn't normally take so long. Perhaps he meant that nonmaterialisation was most relaxing for them; that to entrap people they might put themselves out to perform materialisation; that they personally preferred human bodies to ectoplastic bodies, and ectoplastic bodies to stone and wood bodies of idol format.

Back to Lazarus (Jhn.11). Why was there no mention of darkness, of ectoplasm, or of any gradual building of a body? Because his physical body, only partially decayed, was wrapped in grave clothes and within the

---

[73] Possibly God set up angelic guardians to oversee the spiritual dimension of nations which, sensing the spiritual dimension, set up physical objects, idols, which in turn were used by demons. Hence, poetically put, the elilim ('deities') worshipped by non-Sinai peoples were merely idols, whereas Yahweh had made the heavens (1 Chr.16:26).

---

tomb.[74] And annoyed that Lazarus returned to normal physical life, Jesus' opposition planned his speedy assassination (Jhn.12:10)—hardly shortterm ectoplasm.

What of Samuel (1 Sam.28:11)? Gasson was inconsistent but helpfully renamed the woman from witch to

---

[74]   I smile at Gasson's idea that if Jesus hadn't specified who was to come forth, all the departed—at least in hearing range— would have returned to earthly life, saying "you called?" The operation was done by the Holy Spirit, who would not have tapped each on the shoulder—so to speak. But well, it makes good sermon fodder. As to why Jesus' "be healed", when he didn't specify who was to be healed, didn't heal all folk at least within hearing range, I don't know, if Gasson's idea holds true. Jesus personalised his command because he knew Lazarus personally as a friend, as elsewhere he said "little girl" to a little girl he hadn't known.

More disturbingly, Gasson referred to Jesus as being 'Almighty God' (G142). That is a very dangerous term to use in such an unqualified way, and the NT is softer yet amazingly strong in revealing that *God's son* (the Logos) was *with* deity and *was* deity *yet* became fully human (Jhn.1:1,14). Terms used that in themselves and their context exclude the father and the spirit, can be antitrinitarian: I often quote a *Hillsong* number that says, "you alone are God, Jesus!", which I call hard-Sabellianism (ie one god, one person, three masks), but even Gasson's soft-Sabellianism is still Sabellianism. Moreover, I believe Gasson also tended here to Apollinarianism, the emphasis on Christ's deificity as excluding his humanity. I go back to Mt.12:28—Jesus spoke, but the spirit performed the operations, even as Jesus' non-deific disciples had been able to literally raise those who had recently died, and as we—if given the definite command by the spirit—can.

medium: all the MEVV now nicely do so except, acceptably, the CEV. Some use the term 'ghost', which is probably correct in this context. That she was a genuine medium seems likely enough, and a kindly soul at that. Gasson never attacked Christian Spiritualism as superficially nasty and demonic, but always as superficially nice but demonic: the bait that is fish friendly, is death to the soul.

King Saul was of confused spirituality, he was mentally unstable, and his desperate recourse to a medium was wrong, but his attempt to purge the land of mediums was right. Gasson mentioned such as Lv.20:6: "If any turn to mediums and wizards, prostituting themselves to them, I will set my face against them, and will cut them off from the people" (NRSV)—even sitters were condemned.[75] When sought, Yahweh did not reply to Saul, pending Saul's repentance from a serious sin. But instead of repenting, Saul compounded his disobedience by consulting a medium. It was basically, "If my boss won't answer me, maybe my immediate upliner will". Unfortunately for Saul that upliner had died, but at the séance, he popped up.

---

[75] Elsewhere the death penalty is mandated. Such penalties could pan out as voluntarily leaving the land, being executed, or in some other way being 'cut off'—I suspect sincere repentance would count as death to the occult. Death should also be seen for what it is, namely the termination of mortal life, not the termination of life, and although *murder* is based on sinful attitude and is absolutely sinful, the giver of life is fully entitled to call us off the stage to account for our mortal acts. We all die, and only the pain factor and timing, varies.

Spiritualists might wonder why the anti-medium legislation of Saul had ever been biblical, but they would affirm this woman as a medium, and suggest that she was overwhelmed by such an important spirit. Gasson interpreted the medium's fright differently, besides pointing out that atypically in Spiritualistic circles, the shade was annoyed at being summoned, and sentenced and/or prophesied Saul to imminent death (1 Sam.28:19; 1 Chr.10:13-4).[76] His take (so too John Wesley), was that though the medium was familiar with impersonating spirits, that this time the spirit was genuinely human, and was sent specifically by Yahweh, rather than a demon spirit summoned by herself.[77] Sadly, again Gasson referred to the LORD as Lord, inadvertently downgrading God's name to the Wycliffe/Vulgate level.

---

[76]   Minor point: the last text has a comma instead of a colon (G144).

[77]   That is, a false Samuel would have turned up had the séance gone according to plan, but in an extremely rare move, Yahweh sent the real Samuel to give a stinging rebuke to Saul and a chance for the medium to repent. We could contrast demons impersonating ghosts, to real ghosts, the dead-to-us, who are seldom sent back to the mortal realm. So unlike in Charles Dickens, in the Bible we can read a real ghost story. Some, eg Increase Mather, have argued for a fake-Samuel, pertly because the medium used the term, elohim (1 Sam.28:13), though elohim had a range of meaning including human spirits.

What of Moses and Elijah (Mt.17:1-13//s)?[78] Not least because performing in darkness was certainly much easier in his days, Gasson questioned the assumption that this was an open-air séance. Matthew gave no details of ectoplasm, or of lively songs used to stimulate good vibrations. And what about these visitors from the past? Well, Moses abnormally had had his dead body buried below by Yahweh, whereas Elijah abnormally had had his living body raised above in some tornado-like experience, seemingly bypassing normal death. Both experiences pretty unique—not paradigmatic—which was what the transfiguration was, too![79] The abnormal is hardly the stuff to base any normal séance on. Gasson also noted that like Samuel, Moses and Elijah returned to speak of death.

We could go on. Jesus himself glowed (trans-incarnate glory?); the spirits spoke to *him*—not to any 'sitters'; Peter treated Jesus and the visitors equally in offering to build three rough and ready shelters (do materialised spirits need shelters, and had the spirits not taught Peter about materialisation?); and within moments, the visitors had disappeared and the heavenly voice had spoken.[80]

Gasson could have added that when the resurrected Jesus appeared to Saul of Tarsus, he knocked him

---

[78]   G73 considers this.

[79]   Dt.34:5-6; 2 Kg.2:11

[80]   The deific voice had also spoken at Jesus' water-baptism. Gasson showed elsewhere that that was not an outdoor séance either. Nor was it a séance when on entering Jerusalem the crowd divided over whether they had just heard thunder or an angel (Jhn.12:28-9).

---

down in broad daylight, physically blinded him, and told him to await orders (Ac.9). His travelling companions too were knocked down, saw the terrifying light, and fuzzily heard the voice as thunder. Such were hardly the hallmarks of a séance![81]

I think the big picture is that immediately on death the godly will be enriched (Php.1:21) but not enrobed; released from Earth but not released into deep heaven. I like to picture this as having been on the mortal stage, we become with Christ the audience, and, once the show is finished, we shall depart the earthly theatre, having put on our immortal bodies as outdoor coats, and enrobed thus we will roam the universe, a playground prepared for us by our heavenly father.

---

[81] Formally Ac.9:7 clashes in the KJV with 22:9: Wiki informally and characteristically clashes with Evangelicals, here. Some take the different cases used for ακουω/*akouō* (ie genitive vs accusative), to mean "hearing fuzzily a voice" (φωνη/*phōnē*), noise (9:7), compared to not (ουκ/*ouk*) "unfuzzily hearing a voice" (φωνη/*phōnē*), signal (22:9): John Wesley suggested that that was what Luke had meant.

More likely, thought Daniel Wallace, Luke had heard the story from different sources using *akouō* differently (as it can be) but saying the same thing, and retained their respective wordings: https://books.google.co.uk/books?id=XlqoTVsk2wcC&pg=PA134&redir_esc=y#v=onepage&q&f=false.

Ac.26:13 doesn't say if the sun was shining or not, and, incidentally, lightening can occur in blue skies—bolts *from the blue*. Did Jesus speak in a thunderstorm, with a close shave lightning bolt blinding Paul, and the deific voice in the thunder? See Jhn.12:28-9.

Chapter 13

Trying Spirits

Gasson made the reasonable point that a network that claims its operations to be based on verifiable manifestations, would sink if it lied, but swim if it spoke the truth. Some cults prefer to build on non-falsifiable belief claims, rather than on verifiable phenomena, so can swim in a sea of sheer speculation. With Spiritualism, if every trainee medium is taught how to fake phenomena, one would expect the honest to quit their jobs, especially jobs which result in verifiable deaths and injuries, and which seem to test the honest benevolence of mediums.

Most Spiritualists can spot fake mediums. The real question is not about phenomena but is about their source, the interpretation of their facticity. Scripture speaks against the idea of the deceased being in contact with the mortal realm, and against spirit-guides. Gasson cited 1 Tm.2:5: "God is one; and there is but one mediator between God and humanity, Yeshua the messiah, himself human" (CJB), who speaks by the one spirit. Does God now encourage what he once discouraged? Or what he discouraged then—because mediums were controlled by demons acting nicely—

does he still discourage now—because mediums are still controlled by demons acting nicely?

If the spirits are in sync with God now—whatever they had been in times past—one should expect their messages to align with Scripture. Early on Gasson made a case from the specificity of multiple scriptural messianic prophecies, that Scripture is above the merely divine, standing exclusively as having God as its general editor (my term), not merely as its inspiration.[82] But the messages the spirits give both deviate from, and dismiss, Scripture's message. This conclusion of course might be more challenging to Christian Spiritualists— Gasson's old house—than to Rational Spiritualists, who discount Scripture anyway.

If the spirits are out of sync with God, now—whatever they had been in times past—one should expect their messages to disalign with Scripture. And that, Gasson argued, is precisely what we find. One might expect deceiving spirits to deceive as to the consequences of both disobedience, and of non-obedience, to God. One such line would be to discount the fact of death, such as it being merely a shedding of an evolutionary skin, the standard departure from the mortal realm to

---

[82]   There are naturally better books than his on this, such as Craig Blomberg's ill-titled *Can We Still Believe the Bible?* (2014): Yes Craig, since any ninny *can* believe it for ninny reasons: a child *can* still believe in Santa Claus—and why not? Blomberg meant, *Should We Still Believe the Bible?*, and as a biblical scholar he addressed that question well. Gasson's task here was different, being merely to show that coming to believe that Scripture was in an exclusive way, of God, had merit.

---

something like a Nirvana for souls. Heb.9:27—"we die only once, and then we are judged" (CEV)—be blowed!

Gasson again argued that by blinding folk now—irrespective of their attitude towards God—Satan damns them for eternity. Effectively his picture was of telling lemmings that there is no cliff edge, as they rush forward only to discover it's everlasting hell below. It is not a picture I now hold, but it is a common and effective one in my circles.

My own concern is that Spiritualism binds and blinds in mortal life, damns into missing out God's best in mortal life, gives hell—or at least limbo—on earth, instead of heaven on earth. Its core message also goes under the name of Universalism. It is that all spirits will eventually enjoy the bliss of postmortal life, and in mortal life they need not see Jesus as a saviour, merely as a former medium risen up the spheres, having had his own set of human perfections and imperfections—culturally adjusted. Gasson argued that the stakes were more; I argue that Satan's power is less.

One might assume intelligent spirits could produce ID of those they impersonate, which, Gasson argued, is exactly what we find. We can suffer identity theft even in the secular world. And having gained credence, one might then imagine that they would discuss religion to those interested, or indeed deny it to those who denied it. But a point to note is that when Spiritualists quote Scripture, they are very selective and scant about it, seemingly incapable of sustaining any indepth argument to back their misinterpretations.

Gasson gave numerous examples that show the superficiality of biblical examples cited to support their own claims. He flagged up Augustine as saying that it's the united witness that counts for good teaching, not isolated texts that without their contexts can so easily be twisted. The devil quoted scriptures to Jesus in the wilderness test. For instance, Mt.4:6.

Now taking that in its context and in line with Scripture as a whole, the psalmist was not advising, let alone commanding, anyone to do anything so foolish as to test Yahweh by being a lemming, but implied that if Yahweh commanded his messiah-son into dangerous situations, Yahweh would then provide him with protection within his will, as one loyal to him (Ps.91:9-12): a statement of confidence.

Had Peter stepped out of his boat unbidden, he would have sunk as quickly as a rock—unless God had delivered him from his folly (Mt.14:28). Quoting a few scriptures does not tell us that the speaker is of God. Teachings might be deep without being deeply biblical, and deep philosophy can be spiritually shallow, while the spiritually deep can, philosophically speaking, seem shallow (1 Cor.1:20-5).

Sir Arthur Conan Doyle wrote *The New Revelation*. It covers his conversion to Spiritualism, conversations he had had with spirits, and how they testified that God had now given a New Revelation—which had nothing to do with the cross of Christ. One such spirit happily reported that it had been a Roman Catholic on earth and now lived happily above with spirits from all the world religions, as if differences hadn't mattered.

Another spirit, claiming to have been killed in WW2, 'returned' to assure his 'father' that the whiskey and cigars above were simply divine. Perhaps a rather mundane report from the realms above? Sir Arthur admitted that his New Revelation conflicted with the Old Revelation, indeed that it conflicted most with those who held most rigidly to the Bible, and that he himself had come to think that Christianity was delusional, sadly needing intensive explanation and development to make any sense.[83]

Yahweh's caution to Adam and Eve was twisted by the serpent; likewise, by Spiritualism.[84] That first defeat of humanity was followed up by the defeat of the satan by Jesus, the prophesied human descendant of the woman.[85] I agree with much said by Gasson here, but I don't agree with putting words into God's mouth, so to speak—what I call voxdeism. But I admire his touch of creative genius in basically contrasting a lie—"eat of the tree of Spiritualism and you will surely live"—with the truth—"eat of the tree of Spiritualism and you will surely die". I fully like what he said, without fully liking

---

[83]   I frame this as Sir Arthur's personal standpoint.

[84]   That the Bible and science happily stand together is a point made by many fine books. Christians can usually agree that whether or not we have semi-poetry or literal history here, the Adam/Eve theme is an important theme on which much is meaningfully hung.

[85]   Gasson referred to a dubious text about Jesus sweating drops of blood— but perhaps Lk.22:43-4 should be kept only as a footnote. That people under great stress can seemingly sweat blood in known, but whether the text that says that Jesus did so is biblical, is debateable, and on a technical point, if Luke said this, he also said 'like blood', not 'blood': I suspect that Gasson simply sang in his head C H Gabriel's *I Stand Amazed* song of 1905.

---

how he said it. We should see that there is death in life. Adam and Eve died to God in a profoundly non-physical way that day.

There are also ways in which Christians can die to God's revelation: the Galatians who had died to the gospel, could be resurrected by Paul (Gal.3:1). Speaking of which, Gasson deemed Sir Arthur's New Revelation to be a false gospel: "...even if we or an angel from heaven should preach a gospel other than the one we preached to you, let them be under God's curse!" (NIV: Gal.1:8). Sir Arthur (a bit like Islam) posited that Jesus (as the 'christ spirit') was very high up the spiritual spheres, but that God was far higher than that. The idea would be of Jesus having been simply a great medium—some spirits now being less close, some now closer, to God. This standard teaching in Spiritualism falls short of Jesus as God's son, being God-the-son-incarnate.

Biblically it's not a case of spirit levels, but of Jesus—the human out-raying of God the son into space-time—being lord of the church, and chief of the new humanity that he has created by first defeating death. Spiritualism misidentifies both his ontology and his function, as it gropes in the dark for light. Gasson cited various bits from Spiritualist literature, showing a different gospel which is not really good news.

According to Spiritualism, there was no fundamental rebellion by man against God, so no need to surrender in repentance, no need to be radically changed by him, merely to be enlightened as to a universal upwards trend in spirituality. According to Gasson, Spiritualism is spiritually defiling, and spiritually backward.

He briefly looked at the story of Dives and Lazarus (Dives is a nickname for an unnamed character). I think that this was not a true story about literal people, but was a true story about fictitious characters, in which certain details might be colouring rather than literal fact. I do not think that just because Lazarus was given heaven as recompense for abuse in this life, every abused person will necessarily make heaven (Lk.16:25).

In this story there was some Jewish humour, and simplification as in Negro Spirituals, of reversed lots. The story point is that besides a fundamental divide between heaven and hell, even if the departed could warn former family (the Bible did that), it wouldn't warm human hearts, and showed the hellishness of cold hearts. I think that the story should not be taken literally, but should be taken as showing what biblical teaching had made clear enough, namely that the experience of the covenant people did not include revolving doors between mortal and postmortal lands (2 Sam.12:23). Had that idea been unbiblical, it would never have floated as a Jewish story. Nothing that Jesus taught suggested that a revolving door has since been set up, though he as lord of life can return at will.

Sir Arthur, like many before and after him, never got his head around Jesus' death as being of God's design, an entering death to overcome death for others. For Sir Arthur, we fight our own battles but spirits can be useful allies. Spiritualism fails to grasp the grace of God: the fact that we are valueless to God, yet precious to him; that he needs us not, but has given himself to us for us; that he loves the world, and gave his one-of-a-kind son to save the rebellious world (Jhn.3:16-7).

Spiritualism is a fundamentally comforting, rather than a fundamentally challenging, religion (Jas.1:26-7).

Gasson, trying these spirits by what they said or didn't say, concluded that they fail the biblical test, whereas the Bible does not fail us. Some recommend mediums and necromancers (ESV: Is.8:17), but, Isaiah said, "look to God's instructions and teachings! People who contradict his word are completely in the dark" (Is.8:20), as the NLT puts it, or as the NCV puts it, "you should follow the teachings and your covenant with Yahweh. The mediums and fortune-tellers do not speak the word of Yahweh, so their words are worth nothing" (modified).

Chapter 14

After the Raves

Naturally, church folk will use church-speak. We've all got our own set, and there will be a fair bit of overlap. Sometimes we change our talk—for better or worse. Some parts of Gasson's terminology I once shared. Some parts might now simply benefit from a bit of explanation, especially to non-church folk who don't—whether they should or shouldn't—speak the same lingo. These things aren't crucial to his book, and to front-load them would be to misdirect from Gasson's aim. Perhaps they are specialist issues, better ignored or back-loaded. Since I do not wish to ignore them, I back-load them here.

Artificial Reverence

Capitalising so-called reverential pronouns, such as [Him] instead of [him], began in the C19. This practice, not in the biblical texts, should be either not adopted, or un-adopted. It is ironic that some songwriters add capitals for pronouns of Yahweh/Yeshua, yet remove Tyndale's capitals representing God's actual name— LORD becomes Lord; Yahweh is called Adonai (or

Yeshua). Songwriters, often poor theologians, swallow cultural gnats and strain out biblical camels.[86]

Blood

G12 speaks of being "redeemed by the precious blood of Jesus". G154 speaks of being "blood-washed". Talk of "the blood" caused confusion in Ancient Rome, with some accusing the Christians of literally drinking blood! I have myself written a few Vampire books, but Christians are not vampires, sanguivores! Some even have an issue with Black Pudding, which to them is subjectively a sin (Rm.14:23). The church basically has insider language, which can vary denomination to denomination, tribe to tribe, and over time.

Gasson used *the blood*, to refer to the biblical idea of one creature dying (losing blood symbolised this) to save another by dying in their place. Gasson used *blood-washed*, as meaning redeemed, bought back from the penalty of death by another's death (symbolised as bleeding unto death for us). It is one of a number of biblical pictures to highlight the fact, however pictured, that in the battle Christ had to die if we were to live. Many songs speak of Yeshua's blood.

A linked expression is "pleading the blood" (G29), which means asking God the father to heed those who have come to him through Christ's death. Many, especially non-Christians, object that it all sounds rather barbaric, even of God (if he exists). But here I merely explain what Gasson meant by using such terms.

---

[86]   My *Singing's Gone Global*, covers Christian lyricology.

Broken Body

Irrespective of how Spiritualists may put it, I use the correct term, *given*, rather than the incorrect, *broken*. The medieval *Textus Receptus* tradition still feeds the 'broken body' myth, though not one of his bones was broken (Jhn.19:36)—how can a body be broken without breaking at least one of our 206 bones? "This is my body, [which is] broken for you", is noncanonical, misquoting Jesus. It is a human tradition that never contaminated the Gospel accounts—where one might most expect it to be, had it been genuine—only Paul's. Bread to be shared had to be broken, torn into pieces, indeed some say his body was torn, though not into pieces! Bread signifies several things, such as basic need, and particularly the unleavened flight from slavery to freedom. In the Passover, the lambs' bones were *not* broken (Ex.12:46/Nb.9:12; 1 Cor.5:7; 1 Pt.1:19). This was a sacrifice which all the redeemed shared.

Some say there's no harm in keeping the idea, broken. OK fine, let's say that Jesus said, "my body bled for you". The point is that whether broken or not, if it's not what Jesus said, we shouldn't say that he said it. If we lie if we say that Jesus said that he was the lord of the dance—he did not—do we not lie if we say that Jesus said that his body was broken, since he did not?

Incidentally, breaking bread together, primarily meant sharing a meal: the holy meal they shared spoke of Christ's death (1 Cor.10:16). Some church networks speak of the Eucharist, as a Breaking [of] Bread, but thankfully not as the Breaking [of] Body. The word κλωμενον/*klōmenon*, possibly added by Ambrosiaster (C4), lodged itself into the Greek speaking Byzantine

Empire, and so became the Greek majority word. For 1 Cor.11:24, 𝔓46, ℵ, B, A, and C3 Cyprian of Carthage, all witness to *unbroken*. To soften the scandal of removing the *broken body* myth, some suggest broken *flesh*, *soul*, or *spirit*. Again, however true such might be, Jesus did not say σαρξ/*sarx*, ψυχη/*psuchē*, or πνευμα/*pneuma*, here. Jesus gave his whole body voluntarily to his executioners for us (Lv.1—where burning dramatised that the whole offering had been delivered to Yahweh's domain).

Christ Jesus

Unlike Gasson, many ethnic Jews who convert to Christ, nowadays prefer to speak in national identity terms of *messiah*, and many in other ethnicities are happy to toggle between the terms *messiah* and *christ*.[87] In passing it can be sad yet wise to flag up the

---

[87]   Translation policies range from being reluctant to translate *christos* as other than *christ* (CEB/LEB/NCV/NKJV), to scratching the ethno-Zionizing itch (for which the ISV is far from shy), to completely skipping the term *christ* in favour of *messiah* (CJB).

For ethnic Jews, it can be good to see a more familiar face (*messiah*) turning up more than twice in John's Gospel. But to totally skip the term *christ* for cultural reasons of past bitterness, can be to blinker them to the globality of the church in favour of tunnel vision, and to miss the wood for the tree. Messiah went global; *Saul* became *Paul*. *Christ* is a big historical term with both good and bad baggage.

For new covenant believers at large, it can be good to see a less familiar face (*messiah*) turning up more than twice in John's Gospel. For to completely skip the term *messiah* for cultural reasons of past bitterness, can be to blinker them from the Jewish/Gentile life situation of

---

Sacred Name Movement, which is in a muddle trying to get right the exact name of God the father, and also of God the son in his human mode. The Movement is now in many strands which disagree as to whether the only and must use names, are *Yahowah, Yahvah, Yahwah, Yahweh*, or *Yohwah*, for God the father, and *Yahoshua, Yahshua*, or *Yeshua*, for God the son as human. They agree that only those who get it right avoid blasphemy, so there's a lot at stake.[88] They have gained a little light in turning to the dark side. Far happier and wiser are they who can happily toggle between the terms *Jesus* and *Yeshua*. But to make one or the other an issue, or even to make some third term their denominational flag, is bad.

Christian Descriptors

Gasson used a number of synonymity terms for 'Christian', since roundabout terms can help define what 'Christian' means. That some claim to be

---

the C1 world, and to miss the tree for the wood. Christ came through the ethnic-Jewish tunnel; *Paul* came from *Saul. Messiah* is a big historical term with both good and bad baggage.

I favour *messiah* in contexts where the ethno-Jewish feel was likely. For the Gospels I stand with the CEV/ERV/NABRE/NIV/NLT/NRSV for their functional approach, though they underplay (especially in *Hebrews*) the scope to messianise. For a balanced approach to the NT, here sadly surpassed, the HCSB best hit the mark.

88   Besides a drive to re-Sinaise people—seeking to resurrect what God has crucified (Rm.7:6)—they perhaps overlook that the name *Yahweh* can double for the trinity, deity *in toto*.

Christians who aren't, and that some who bring shame to Christ are (but we would not wish others to know it!), should be kept in mind. Sad realities.

<u>Children of God</u> Some use this to mean all human beings—children of Adam—and there is even a Christian-identity cult that has claimed that name, though it has officially shed that name it tainted. In my Hull days I was unsuccessfully fished by a rather attractive flirty fisher of that cult. But while the term may be used of all human beings (God's 'creational' fatherhood), and perhaps even extends to nonhuman spirits (*Job* 1:6: αγγελοι/*angeloi* in the Greek), in Gasson's book it simply means 'Christians'.

<u>New Creatures in Christ</u> This is taken from 2 Cor.5:17 in many older versions. 'Creations' is generally used to update. But there is some ambivalence—perhaps intentional—in Paul's text: perhaps he wished to include both the idea of Christians *being* essentially new creations and *being within* the new messianic creation, showing that the new age had dawned.[89]

<u>Born-Again</u> This term is loved and loathed. Some use it for 'true', as opposed to 'nominal-only', Christians. Radical proponents insist that the only true Christians

---

[89]   "The translation 'there is a new creation', would mean that the new creation does not merely involve the personal transformation of individuals but encompasses the eschatological act of recreating humans and nature in Christ. It would also include the new community, which has done away with the artificial barriers of circumcision and uncircumcision (Gal.6:15-6; see Eph.2:14-6) as part of this new creation" David E Garland's *2 Corinthians* (NAB), 1999:5959-63 of 19890.

are Born-Again Christians. Radical opponents can say that any type of Christian is fine except the Born-Again loonies. Years ago, my reply to the question, "Are you a Born-Again Christian?" shocked a questioner. I replied that "that's the only kind there is." I was in fact both right and wrong. Right, in that there is only one kind of Christian, in the same sense that there is only one form of white light, though many variations within that spectrum. Wrong, in that biblically speaking, the term Born-Again is what Nicodemus, not Jesus, said playfully—and Jesus said that that was daft.

Their friendly dialogue was in three parts. Jesus served up an ambiguous *born anew* (CEB). Smiling, Nicodemus returned a 'you cannot be serious' *born again?* (ERV/NCV/NLT/Wycliffe), to which Jesus volleyed with *spiritual birth*, you ninny (CEV/LEB/NRSV). [90] Game, set, and match. Nicodemus remained an honest spectator until Yeshua fought and defeated Death, revealing himself as heaven's champion.

Church

The English word *church* comes from a Greek word κυριακου/*kuriakou*, meaning something that belongs to a lord. Since its context is God's appointed lord, Yeshua, Gasson was dead wrong to use it for Spiritualist premises, whatever State registration might buy into. Call them Spiritualist *assemblies*,

---

[90]   Comparative grades: CEB/NRSV (A+); CEV/NABRE (A); LEB (B+); ERV/NCV/NLT/NIV (D); NKJV (D-).
Incidentally, *born again* shouldn't be used in 1 Pt.1:23. There the KJV ditched the Reformation's Tyndale (born anew) in favour of Rome's Martin (born again).

congregations, but don't call them *churches*, for that title's been bought by precious blood. Incidentally a Greek word for congregation/assembly, is εκκλησια/ *ekklēsia*, and has long been translated by the English 'church'—eg 'chyrcan' in the 1175 West Saxon translation. Tyndale rebranded it as *congregation*, but even against the Bishops' the KJV reverted back to 'church' under the pressure of the Geneva and Douay-Rheims versions, and King James.

Correctly, Gasson used "the Church of Christ" and "the Church of God" interchangeably, not as subsections of the church, but as the church globally over the millennia. I think that those who use them happily as denominational tags, use them sinfully, even blasphemously, in that we abuse the words of our lord: "I will build my church" (Mt.16:18)—one church. Biblically, there is only one global church, though many denominations, and many local churches/ congregations exist.

My own solution to the current mess would be a repentant and a radical renaming exercise globally. This would undoubtedly cause problems, even as surgery causes disruption. Bureaucratic re-registrations would involve legal hassle, and Christians would have to adjust to rethinking, howbeit to biblical thinking. We could use [Church] as a standard prefix, followed by a denominational label. For example, [Roman Catholic Church] could be renamed [Church:Roman]; [Orthodox Church] could become Church:Orthodox; [Church of the Nazarene] could relabel as Church:Nazarene; [Methodist Church] rebrand as Church:Methodist, etc. Rejigging labels would obviously take some time, humility, and liaison, across the board, and realistically most might prefer the words of Aslan: "Peace.... All names will soon be restored to their proper owners" (C S Lewis' *The Lion, the Witch, and the Wardrobe*, ch.13). But I would like to think that when messiah returns, he will find church faithfulness: *Revelation* urged local churches to repent, changing their wrong hearts, their wrong thinking, and their wrong actions/inactions, rather than waiting for him to return and remove their local light.

Gender

Gasson's book speaks of 'man/men' in an inclusive, not an exclusive, sense, as befitted his cultural norm. Languages can have gender waves. English has sometimes used 'men' to mean 'adult human(s)', and sometimes only to mean 'adult male human(s)' (D A Carson's *The Inclusive Language Debate*). Gasson's 'wave' is receding, so can have flinch value to today's women and children, so ideally should be updated.

God's Name

Ethnic Israel's sin led to her sense of guilt, shame, and fear to pronounce God's name. Avoidance included speaking 'Lord' (*Adonai*) in place of God's name in the Hebrew, and in the Greek translation writing 'lord' (κυριος/*kurios*). Note, though of inconsistent quality, the Greek ('Septuagint/LXX') used 'lord' rather than '*the* lord', to keep the idea of a personal name rather than a title. Similarly, in his schoolboy years, the actor Jack Lord was probably known as Lord, but not as *the* lord.

The KJV benefited from Tyndale, who had gently restored the idea of God's name into English. Gasson's book uses the KJV, but by ditching Tyndale, changed LORD to Lord—a common copy/paste or scribal error: "the LORD" takes us away from God's name, but "the Lord" takes us further away, and is even less biblical.[91]

I seek to adhere to Paul's careful distinction between [lord] and [God], and cringe at talk about us being children of *the lord* (G90): we must never speak of Jesus the lord having children—we are children of God the father. But do any actually call Jesus their father? Yes, some even sing it. Chris Bowater even wrote a song to the spirit as to his father (Holy Spirit, We Welcome You (1986)): "let the breeze of your presence blow / that your children here might truly know." It's right to welcome the spirit, but not as being our father, nor to welcome Jesus as being our sister. We are heirs of the father, and co-heirs with his son; Jesus, unashamed to call us his brothers and sisters, is probably ashamed to be called our father. Clear blue water between the terms *God* and *lord*, will help attain/maintain trinitarian sanity (see my *Singing's Gone Global*).

Jew

The term *Israel*, began with one person, was bequeathed to his sons, and formed an ethnic race, which in time divided into Israelites to the north, and Judahites to the south. After the north disappeared, the overall name *Israel* seeped back into the Judahites, helping the terms Jew and Israeli[te] to more or less be taken as synonyms today. I cover this more fully in my *Israel's Gone Global*. The term Jew is too often taken in

---

[91]   Comparative grades: LEB (A+); ERV (D+); NLT/NABRE (D); NRSV/CEB/CEV/NCV/NIV/NKJV (D-).

a nonbiblical way to denote a religion somehow possessed by—and possessing—the ethnic race of Jews. Gasson merely went along with the crowd on this. Thus...

- "being a Jew was part of my duty" (G17). I might as well say that being an Englishman is part of my duty.
- "deciding whether I was a Jew or a Christian" (G17). I might as well "decide whether I am an Englishman or a Christian."

This category error goes way back: Shakespeare's Shylock even suffered from it! A further complication is that Christians are, by biblical definition, *Jews*, true Israelites of the true, intended, Jacob/Israel. Among the many texts showing this, in *Galatians* Paul used symbolism to say that his ethnic people, if believing themselves ethnically to be spiritually Sarah/freed from sin, were in fact spiritually Hagar/slaves to sin (Gal.4:21ff.), and that corporately it was the true circumcision, Christians, who were spiritually Sarah.

When the Bible uses evil terms of messiah-rejecting Jews, it implies them to be equal to, but not worse than, the global κοσμος/*kosmos* (God-hostile humanity)—spiritually *goyim* whose 'god' is Satan (2 Cor.4:4). The irony is that ethnic Israel/Jewry, having under Sinai been distinct from the *goyim* (Gentiles), has after Sinai become fellow Gentiles unawares. One can be an Arab (race) and a *Judaist* (religion). One can be an ethnic *Jew* (race) and a Muslim (religion). One can be a Hindustani (race) and an Atheist (religion). One can be an Apache (race) and a Christian (religion). 'Christian or Jew?' is a category error: belief need not coincide with blood.

Minister

Biblically a minister is basically a servant. When I went to Wigan for a church interview, Ray Belfield asked if I believed in Christian women's ministry. I was happy to say Yes, since every Christian is a servant and so every Christian man, women, and child, should serve. There is biblical scope for some ministers/servants to specialise with a local church setting, and from the word for minister (διακονος/*diakonos*) we have the terms *deacon*, and *diaconate* (group of deacons), effectively specialist servants of general servants. *Minister* can also function as a common church label for church leaders, sometimes to avoid the term *priest*. Some secular leaders also have the title, Minister, and I do not begrudge it to Spiritualists.

Polytheism

"My god" is a common expression in Christian circles, and some people use it as an expletive for amazement or contempt. Muslims speak of the Christian god; Christians talk of the Islamic god. Since both sides say that there is only one god, this does not compute. Christianity and Islam have different *concepts* about God, not different *gods*.

Nowadays I drop my/our/your-god terms. Translating one language into another involves being honest to the source language. And also realising that the idioms—ways of expression—of the target/receptor languages, can be very different, and being honest to the target language. Poetical language can be turned into philosophical, and *vice versa*.

The Old Testament (Tanak) spoke frequently in polytheistic language, since it spoke to its students. It bears copious witness to immature and unsettled thinking on this, with Yahweh often assumed by his students to be the best optional god/deity for them (henotheism).[92]

I hold that the NT achieved a sturdy monotheism—though with some inconsistency of wording—nevertheless showing poetical links to the class of Sinai. Perhaps in some missionary circles—the church began within pluralism—the language of polytheism might still be a suitable starting point. After all, Paul could begin in a your-god style, then demolish that idea as outdated by the advent of Christ (eg Ac.17:23-31).

For translation, I would keep all OT polytheistic style use, put in lowercase (ie god, not God as some reverential noun), to underline the older lessons,[93] and where polytheistic style has entered into the NT (exempting perhaps OT citations), employ workarounds to translate into its upgraded framework. It can be done; some

---

[92]   I prefer this term to *monolatry* (worship of one god), since it incorporates monolatry but allows the then accepted idea that other deities (gods/goddesses) might exist. I accept that there were flashes of monotheism within the Tanak, which rejected the 'gods' of the nations as merely so-called gods/goddesses, mere idols.

[93]   The earlier class were not taught that there was only one god, but that for them Yahweh was the only god to trust and be loyal to, him being their covenant god. They were tested on how well that lesson of trust and loyalty was learnt within that framework. Some students saw, and wrote of, the bigger picture.

versions do it better than others; none are flawless.[94] I cringe whenever I hear fellow believers describe our-kind-of-god being good, loving, whatever. Good heavens, what other kinds of gods are there?

Some examples:

- "to the only wise god", to "to God, alone wise" (Rm.16:27)
- "God is not a god of disorder", to "God wants everything to be done...in order" (1 Cor.14:33)
- "our god and father", to "God our father" (Gal.1:4)
- "the god of peace", to "God, who gives peace" (Php.4:9)

Prayer Direction

Some use 'lord' both to refer to God—Tyndale often translated God's name as the LORD—and to Jesus, lord to the glory of God. Used thus, 'lord' can function misleadingly as a bridging term. It is safer not to "pray to the lord", if that means asking Jesus for anything. The problem is that the general biblical rule is that we are neither to ask Jesus nor the spirit for things, but only our heavenly father.

Too easily, otherwise, we begin praying to God the father in terms of 'lord', and before we know it, we're thanking the same 'lord' for dying for us: God as God did not die for us, though Jesus, God the son as a human being, did. When our devotional life runs on this level of confusion, our doctrinal life often runs on confused lines too. I find it painful to frequently hear

---

94   Comparative grades: CEV (A+); NLT (B); NCV (D+); ERV/NABRE/NKJV (D); CEB/LEB/NIV/NRSV (D-).

shoddy public prayers—some are sung—proclaiming the shoddy ideas of Sabellianism and Patripassianism. Through such shoddy praying, good church leaders even teach their congregations the basic idea that deity is like one stage actor, switching masks to play three parts, as if the crucified son was the father crucified. Sub-trinitarian praying and thinking is rife in many church circles. Seldom if ever should we use the term 'lord' for God.

Spiritualism

Gasson's second chapter makes in abundantly clear that Gasson rode with the term 'Spiritualism' as the official, convenient, and incorrect, label. He argued that Spiritist-ism was correct. Terms are important to carry intended messages: the occult can sound spiritual and godly, and the homosexual can sound gay and happy. One must always look behind semantic spin—advertising terms—spun for political clout. Had the Movement called itself Spiritual, instead of Spiritualism, it would have been even more contentious, implying that to be spiritual you had to join. As it stands, I have conceded that this term is here to stay and might as well be used, though flagged up as a challenging counterfeit.

Gloria in excelsis Deo

Selective Index

(In paperback format only)

Books by this Author
Theology

Israel's Gone Global

Israel's Gone Global traces salvation through the term, Israel. Was the covenant with the people-nation of Yakob-Yisrael, crossed out? How eternal is covenant? To examine that, we examine marriage. Can a covenant partner be truly divorced? Has Yeshua-Yisrael mediated a spiritual covenant with a spiritual Israel? Is evangelism of ethnic Jews needless, a priority, or neither?

No one could have everlasting life but for the cross, but has it always been globally accessible? Might any who die as Atheists, Hindus, or Islamists, make heaven? And is eternal life joyful? Is everlasting life fun?

Tackling the question of people who die in infancy (or as adults who never heard the gospel), we consider whether it is fair if only those who don't die in infancy get a chance of eternal damnation (if infant universalism), or alone get a chance of eternal heaven (if infant damnation). Does predilectionism make best sense of biblical revelation?

Opportunities to enjoy eternal life spring from the new covenant—reasons to rejoice. But what about salvation history before that covenant?

∞

Singing's Gone Global

Singing's Gone Global, briefly explores the background of singing, before and into ancient Israel. It examines the impact songs have on those who sing, and on those who listen, touching on spiritual warfare. It looks at how nonsense songs neither make sense to evangelism, nor to the evangelised, and asks, "Is there a mûmak in the room?"

Oddly some songwriters simply misunderstand prayer. Part two covers the basics of the trinity, focusing on the spirit in order to understand types of prayer (eg request, gratitude, adoration, chat), leading in turn to a better understanding of our heavenly father, our brother, our helper, and ourselves in Christ's likeness.

Next we look at some common problems. Part three focuses on problems such as buddyism, decontextualising, misvisualisation, and unitarianism. Diagnosis can help Christ's 'bride' to recover from suboptimal and unbiblical songs (Eph.5:18-30).

Giving a Problem Avoidance Grade (PAG)—an A+ to Unsatisfactory scale—in part four we examine specific songs. Weapons forged (Part three), the mûmakil can be attacked, seeking to save and be saved.

Subsequently the book concludes by showing how Christmas carols may be tweaked to better serve our weary world, rejoicing that joy to the world has come.

∞

The Word's Gone Global

The Word's Gone Global, examines Bible text (trusted by early Islam) and introduces textual critique. It looks at the Eastern Orthodox Bible and the Latin Vulgate. Did the Reformation improve text and translation? Were Wycliffe, Tyndale, and Martin, helpful?

Why did the New International Version begin, and why does it enrage? Why did complementarians Don Carson and Wayne Grudem, clash? Is marketing hype between formal and functional equivalence, meaningless? Which version or versions should you regularly read?

In English-speaking circles, Broughton wished to burn Bancroft's King James Version, yet many KJV proponents—think Gail Riplinger and Peter Ruckman—wish to burn all alternatives. More heat than light?

Grade Charts cover 30+ English versions on issues such as God's name, God's son's deity, marriage, gender terms, anti-polytheism, and various issues in John's Gospel. No, Tyndale was not 'born again'. No, John was not antisemitic. No, he did not disagree with the other Gospels.

∞

Prayer's Gone Global

Prayer's Gone Global, begins with ancient civilisations and prayer (the Common Level). Then it narrows into Ancient Israel and prayer (the Sinai Level). Then it deepens and widens into Global Israel and prayer (the Christian Level). Deity is revealed as trinity: Sabellians mislead.

Relating to the trinity includes the Holy Spirit. We should of course work with him, but should we worship him, complain to him, chat with him? Above the spirit stands the often forgotten father—oh let Jesusism retire.

Authority is another issue. Are we authorised to decree and declare? Is binding and loosing actually prayer, or is it evangelism? Is it biblical never to command miracles? Do we miss out on the supernatural which Jesus modelled for us, too fearful of strange fire to offer holy fire?

You can freshen up your prayer life—ride the blessed camel, not the gnats. Listen to Saint Anselm pray, and C S Lewis and 'Malcolm' discuss prayer, and be blessed.

∞

Revelation's Gone Global

Revelation's Gone Global, is a telling of John's future, as if by a then contemporary named Sonafets speaking to his church about how John's apocalyptic scroll related to their days, and about what was still future to John.

Encouragement is a big theme. Roman persecution was an unpredictable beast which ferociously lashed out here and there—what church or Christian was safe? But God stood behind the scenes, allowing but limiting their enemy, and messiah walked among the churches, lights to the world.

Victory lay neither with Rome nor demons, but with God, and with the warrior lamb who had been slain. Victory was guaranteed, and would finally be enjoyed.

Exhortation was given to believers, to play their part while on the mortal stage. They were to walk in the light, and not to let the show down by straying.

Angels of power, actively working out God's will, far exceed the puny forces against God and his church. His wrath was not pleasant, but could be redemptive until the new age begins.

C S Lewis' essay, The World's Last Night, is briefly examined to enjoin a calm awareness of the ongoing battle we are in, and the brightness to come when the king returns.

∞

The Father's Gone Global

Focusing from God as father, to the specific person of God the father, The Father's Gone Global looks at the biblical parent/child pattern from Genesis, through Sinai, and into the Church.

Abba as a new covenant word expresses deep filial affection even under deep anguish in our Gethsemane battles. Coming through God's belovèd son, it speaks into the church and into our lives.

Though to many the 'forgotten father', human parents/fathers should 'put on' God the father, and his children should 'put on' his son. We forget him to our cost.

Human applications aside, what is the Eternal Society? Is filial relationship modelled by God the son incarnate? Are we to be always obedient to our father and guided by the spirit?

Eschatologically the father will be supreme, but even now he is the one to whom the son points. Christian life should relate to God our father, God our brother, and God our helper, prioritising the father.

Renewal of the church is vital for our confused world, but renewal which downplays the father falls short of the good news which Christ created and the spirit circulates. May this book play its part.

∞

Salvation Now and Life Beyond

Salvation Now, divides the doctrine of salvation into the four main levels of common humanity, the old covenant, the new covenant, and life beyond.

A big weight is put on the term, Israel, as God's master plan. This too has four levels, meaning a man, a people, a new man, and a new people, respectively.

Various ideas of what Christianity, the new covenant for the new people, is good for, and how we get into it and best enjoy it, are examined, and a faith-based inexclusivism is suggested.

Everlasting life is seen as the ultimate goal of salvation, universal meaningfulness and love beyond all fears and pains.

∞

Revisiting

Revisiting The Challenging Counterfeit

Revisiting The Challenging Counterfeit, is an extended review of Raphael Gasson's 'The Challenging Counterfeit' (1966). Raphael was an ethnic Jew whose spiritual journey included many years as a Christian Spiritualist minister.

Today, when psychic phenomena captures the imagination and the bank accounts of popular media, it is useful to unearth the witness of one who had well worn the T-shirt of a medium with pride, only to bury it in unholy ground as a thing of shame and of sorrow and of wasted time.

Challengingly, his book exposes what true Spiritualism is. He had nothing but high praise for Spiritualists, and deep condemnation for Spiritualism. For he had discovered true Spiritualism to be itself a fake of true Spirituality, a mere Counterfeit that, in deposing death in the mind, enthroned it in the soul.

Counterfeit phenomena covered include apparitions, Rescue Work and haunted houses, materialisation of pets, psychic healing, Lyceums, clairvoyance, and OOBEs—to name but a few. This book surveys his exposé of Spiritualism's offer of fascinating fish bait, false food falling short of real food for the soul. Though it takes issue with Raphael on a number of points, his core insights are powerful and timely, helping us to avoid—or escape from—a Challenging Counterfeit, and to discover true spiritual currency.

∞

Revisiting The Pilgrim's Progress

Revisiting The Pilgrim's Progress, is a re-dreaming of John Bunyan's most famous dream. An ex-serviceman and ex-jailbird, he found fortune, freedom, and fans worldwide.

This dream journey is substantially Bunyan's from this world, and into that which is to come. It is not a fun story, but it has lots of danger, and joy, and reflection on some big life themes.

Profoundly, sinners who become pilgrims become saints. But that can make life more difficult. One big question is, Is it worth it? One big temptation is, Turn back or turn aside. And if you see others do so, that makes it harder not to. Bunyan was tempted. And he discovered that not deserting, can lead to despair. But he also discovered a key to liberty.

Pre-eminently, it is a story of grace which many follow. Grace begins the journey, helps along the way, and brings the story to a happily ever after. Are all fairy stories based on heaven?

∞

Fantasy

The Simbolinian Files

From Simboliniad, a crystal planet long gone, came the vampire race, the wapierze, thelodynamic shapeshifters seeking blood. Most oppose Usen, King of the Light, so side with the Necros. Seldom do the Guardians intervene. These files, secretly secured from various insider sources, reveal something of what they have done, and will do.

∞

Vampire Redemption

Artificial intelligence, created by superpowers to save man, questions man's worth, and becomes The Beast. Escaping into the wild, many discover a wilderness infested by zombies and diabolical spirits. Who will help? Father Doyle? He's tied up with the mysterious Lilith. Tariq? He's tied up with Wilma. Can the bigoted old exorcist deliver him from evil?

Radical problems can require radical solutions. But does man really need hobs, elves, and the more ancient of days? In the surrounding shadows, vampires and demons form an alliance, raising the stakes against Whitby and Tyneside. Powerful vampires live shrouded within Whitby, speaking of life beyond this galaxy. Is salvation in the stars? Is Sunniva, the despised woman of Alban, worth dying for? Big questions, needing big answers. Not even Guardian Odin can foretell man's fate and, as silent stars go by, one little town must awake from its dreams.

Though The Beast slumbers purposeless and undisturbed, in the far west a global giant slowly opens its yellow eyes and threatens to smother the earth in fire and ice. There is one chance only.

∞

Vampire Extraction

Bitterly long their imprisoned spirits lay, fast bound to Earth's drowsy decay. To the Simbolinian race, there was no hell on Earth, for Earth was hell, and Usen the cosmic jailer. Was it so surprising that as vampires they stalked Usen's children for blood? Most chose the Kingdom of Night, wary of both the Kingdom of Necros and the Kingdom of Dawn.

As queen of the Night, Lilith's story streams through the summer sands of Sumer, and through the green woods of Sherwood. It flags up both dishonour and joy, and cuts across the paths of Ulrica the Saxon and Robin the Hood, as tyrannies rise and fall in merry England. Bigotry seldom has a good word to say about Usen, nor about mercy. Reluctantly, Lilith examines what it means to show mercy, to show weakness. Wulfgar had enslaved Ulrica: is it mercy to let her burn; should mercy have spared Lona? Could

Hamashiach turn daughter into sister? Could Count Dracula be turned from his madness? Has Draven really betrayed his mother? Life has many questions.

Tales picture ideas, letting us walk through the eyes of others to better see ourselves. This story exposes subplots behind common history. How these chronicles came to be written up is, in the spirit confidentiality, not for the public eye. What truth is within you must judge. Discrimination is a gift from Beyond, from which the words still echo: mercy is better than sacrifice. Indeed mercy can be sacrifice. Judge well.

∞

Vampire Count

Vampires were not always earthbound, nor are all evil, but being victims of Usen's Eighth Law, his Children became their fair game. Yet the Night Kingdom was divided: some veered to the Necros; some to the Dawn. Who was wrong; who was right?

Long ago one incited his people to racial violence against elven and human kinds. Ever he strove to be king of the Night, and unto Necuratu the Dark Lord he gave the dragon shape. He made war upon the ancient Middle East, even the Nephilim War. Against him the Light raised flood and division.

At last his own people, paying the price of his rampage, bound him in deep sleep. Yet the millennia seemed meaningless to him: even the rising of Hamashiach hardly disturbed his dreams. At last awoken, he and his brides stalked the hills of Transylvania. Only the fear of Lilith—and after her unforgivable sin, Queen Rangda—chained their bloodlust.

Dracula sought escape and autonomy. By cunning and devious means, he immigrated to London via Whitby. Pursuit followed swiftly, with a shadowminder helping a circle of human headhunters, though they sought the death of all vampires.

∞

Vampire Grail

Wulfgar is a vampire, a thelodynamic creature from another galaxy, now locked into our world by one called the Cosmic Jailer. He hides a tormenting secret from his queen, Lilith, which the Necros use as blackmail. She will only go so far with the Necros against Hamashiach—Wulfgar must go further.

Unknown to the Darkness, to bury Hamashiach is to plant the Light. From the buried seed springs life, and humanity must reimagine itself. Longinus turns to The Way, the nexus of the Seventh Age. His spear goes on a special mission to the island of Briton, where Wulfgar lives again.

Logres is centred on Avalon, but raises up Arthur, a man of mixed race, to carry its flag and to protect against the Saxons. But its main enemy is the Darkness, which ever seeks to extinguish the Light it hates and fears.

Finally, it seems as if the Darkness has won, and the dark ages descend. But does the Light not shine in the Darkness? Must Wulfgar remain in the Night?

∞

Vampire Shadows

Dark vampires, hidden within the ancient empire of Khem, fall out with the king who, stirred up by the Necros, enslaves the Sheep People. But Iahveh, the shepherd-divinity, is stirred up, and stirs up a hidden hero to force a way out.

Apprehensively the two vampire-magicians join the Sheep of Iahveh, on their long and deadly trek in search of a promised land. Can any survive?

Warily they ask deep questions. Is Usen evil, as prejudice says? Is he possibly a good jailer? Are his unusual regulations, meaningful? They risk ending up in death.

Neverendingly the Sheep's sorry story drags out in interminable peregrination. Weary of wandering, most would settle for some green pastures and untroubled waters. But as they well know, that would take a miracle.

www.ingramcontent.com/pod-product-compliance
Lightning Source LLC
Chambersburg PA
CBHW061739020426
42331CB00006B/1291